THE REFERENCE

Volu

No.

3. Representative American Speeches: 1944-1945. A. C. Baird. $1.25.
5. Anatomy of Racial Intolerance. G. B. de Huszar. $1.25.
6. Palestine: Jewish Homeland? J. E. Johnsen. $1.25.

Volume XVII

No.

4. Representative American Speeches: 1943-1944. A. C. Baird. $1.25.
5. Lowering the Voting Age. J. E. Johnsen. $1.25.

Volume XVI

No.

1. Representative American Speeches: 1941-1942. A. C. Baird. $1.25.
2. Plans for a Postwar World. J. E. Johnsen. $1.25.
6. Representative American Speeches: 1942-1943. A. C. Baird. $1.25.
7. Reconstituting the League of Nations. J. E. Johnsen. $1.25.

Volume XV

No.

1. Representative American Speeches: 1940-1941. A. C. Baird. $1.25.
2. Universal Military Service. R. E. Summers and H. B. Summers. $1.25.
3. Federal Regulation of Labor Unions. J. V. Garland. $1.25.
6. Wages and Prices. R. E. Summers. $1.25.
7. The Closed Shop. J. E. Johnsen. $1.25.
9. Permanent Price Control Policy. J. E. Johnsen. $1.25.
10. A Federal Sales Tax. E. R. Nichols. $1.25.

Volume XIV

No.

1. Representative American Speeches: 1939-1940. A. C. Baird. $1.50.
2. Interstate Trade Barriers. J. E. Johnsen. $1.25.
6. Compulsory Military Training. J. E. Johnsen. $1.25.
8. International Federation of Democracies. J. E. Johnsen. $1.25.
9. Debate Index. Supplement. J. E. Johnsen. 75c.

Volume XIII

No.

4. Europe: Versailles to Warsaw. R. S. Kain. $1.25.
5. Public Housing in America. M. B. Schnapper. $1.25.
6. United States Foreign Policy (Supplement) J. E. Johnsen. 75c.
9. The National Labor Relations Act. Should It Be Amended? J. E. Johnsen. $1.25.
10. Trade Unions and the Anti-Trust Laws. J. E. Johnsen. $1.25.

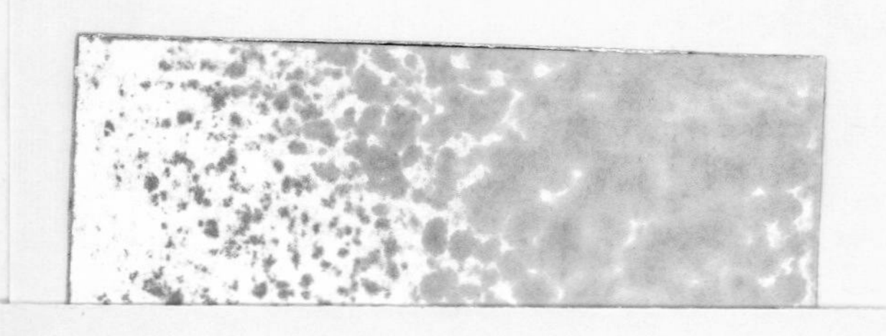

THE REFERENCE SHELF

Vol. 23 No. 4

AMERICA'S WEAPONS OF PSYCHOLOGICAL WARFARE

Edited by

ROBERT E. SUMMERS

THE H. W. WILSON COMPANY
NEW YORK 1951

PREFACE

In the latter part of 1950, the United States Department of State publicly charged that the Soviet Union, as evidenced by a number of actions, was threatening to engage in all-out psychological warfare. The unceasing propaganda campaign being waged by the Soviet Union, its satellite states, and the Communist parties of the democratic nations of the world—directed more and more toward the United States—was proof in itself that America needed to take stock of its assets and liabilities, to redirect its information program toward dynamic counter-propaganda. From every side, the basis of this reorientation was becoming more and more obvious. The question was one of survival—not merely of the survival of the democratic nations of Western Europe and elsewhere, but of the United States itself.

This volume is not intended to supply the answers, nor to provide a technical analysis of the present progam being conducted by the United States. It is, however, a round-up of the best available material, in the opinion of the editor, describing current operations of the United States Information Service and its effectiveness. Perhaps some of the suggestions for improvement which are included here may point to increased effectiveness of the entire program. But the primary purpose of this compilation is to explain what the present program is set up to do, and the manner in which it attempts to do it, with some attention to the success to date of our efforts.

The editor wishes to express sincerest appreciation for the assistance of Representative John Vorys of Ohio, member of the House Committee on Foreign Affairs; of Mr. John Howe, assistant to Senator William Benton of Connecticut; of Senator Tom Connally of Texas, chairman of the Senate Foreign Relations Committee; and of Mr. C. C. O'Day, Clerk of the Senate Committee. Further appreciation is due Professor Sidney Hook and Representative Brien McMahon and to the Foreign Policy Association for their kind permission to use copyrighted materials included in this volume.

Sincerely appreciated also was the cooperation of the editors of the *Academy of Political Science Proceedings*, *American Scholar*, Baltimore *Sun*, *Billboard*, *Changing Times*, *Congressional Digest*, *Editorial Research Reports*, *Educational Screen*, *Foreign Policy Bulletin*, *Fortune*, *Harper's Magazine*, *Nation's Business*, *News Bulletin*, New York *Herald Tribune*, New York *Times*, *Presbyterian Life*, *Public Opinion Quarterly*, *Public Relations News*, *Variety*, *Vital Speeches of the Day*, and *World Affairs*.

ROBERT E. SUMMERS

October 1, 1951

PREFACE

CONTENTS

CURRENT STRATEGY IN THE WAR OF IDEAS

Proof of Effectiveness of the Campaign of Truth

Critical Evaluations of the Propaganda Effort

PROPOSALS FOR MORE EFFECTIVE TACTICS

APPENDIX

APPENDIX

PSYCHOLOGICAL WARFARE: AMERICAN BACKGROUND

EDITOR'S INTRODUCTION

To the casual observer of the world situation, the term "psychological warfare" might seem to have appeared rather suddenly in discussions of foreign policy. Particularly does this seem true when the information service of the Department of State is now labeled as one of "America's weapons of psychological warfare."

It is an interesting paradox that, in creating the information service as a permanent agency of the State Department, the enabling act (Smith-Mundt Act, Public Law 402, 80th Congress) specified only the objectives of promoting "a better understanding of the United States in other countries, and to increase mutual understanding between the people of the United States and the people of other countries." Among the means to be used were an information service "to disseminate abroad information about the United States, its people, and policies promulgated by the Congress, the President, the Secretary of State and other responsible officials of government having to do with matters affecting foreign affairs," and an educational exchange service.

But while this act provided the statutory basis for America's psychological warfare program of today, that does not seem to have been its intent. There is no mention of psychological warfare in the original Smith-Mundt Act or in any amendments to that act. Then what is the source of the current emphasis upon psychological warfare? Why should psychological warfare now assume so much importance?

The answer is not in the information program itself, but in developments abroad. And as a basis for understanding what has taken place in the overseas information picture since 1948 when the Smith-Mundt Act was passed, it is necessary to review briefly the American attitudes toward psychological warfare, propaganda, information, and the previous experience with these implements of national policy.

First of all, what is meant by psychological warfare? Originally it meant "warfare psychologically waged," as the Nazis termed it. In its barest essentials it was merely the application of psychology on a grand scale to military objectives. In Germany, the Nazis experimented with psychological techniques and achieved most of their goals prior to 1941 through such techniques. They gave psychological warfare almost equal status with military warfare in their conquest of Europe. In fact, they built their war strategy around four major weapons: psychological warfare, economic warfare, political warfare, and as a last resort, military warfare. To the Nazi theorists, psychological warfare went on before, during, and after any military action, and its aim was to weaken the enemy, the "divide and conquer" strategy, and to influence public opinion in neutral countries. In essence, it was the use of propaganda against an enemy, together with whatever other measures might be necessary to supplement propaganda.

This brings up the question of what is meant by "propaganda." The definition apparently in favor with the armed services today is that given by Major Paul M. A. Linebarger in the Senior Reserve Officers Training Corps Manual covering "Psychological Warfare":

> Propaganda consists of the planned use of any form of public or mass-produced communication designed to affect the minds and emotions of a given group for a specific public purpose, whether military, economic, or political.

A somewhat narrower definition applies to propaganda in the military sense—that which is directed against "a given enemy, neutral, or friendly group for a specific strategic or tactical purpose." It was this definition which governed the official overseas propaganda of the United States during World War II, and profoundly influenced much of the thinking toward propaganda usage since that time.

Since psychological warfare—together with military propaganda—was engaged in by the United States only in wartime, the tendency was to consider it purely a wartime measure. Once the war ended, so did the psychological warfare agencies. Even the leading authorities on the subject, who were active in the psychological warfare agencies during the war, have tended to write only in terms of wartime uses and experiences. With minor exceptions, little attention has been given to psychological warfare as a peacetime program of action for the United States.

True, it was recognized that more information about the United States was needed abroad, that diplomacy was no longer the prerogative of statesmen, and that the postwar world would be governed by "people speaking to people." This meant a more fully and accurately informed public opinion on international affairs. The aims and objectives of the United States needed to be stated fully and to be reported honestly abroad. That was a commonly accepted philosophy. But within a matter of months after the end of World War II it was discovered that the extent of foreign distrust and misunderstanding was alarming. Even extensive economic aid and outright gifts were winning few friends for the United States abroad. The reason is now past history. Natural fears and disillusionment were being fed by Communist propaganda on a scale almost beyond comprehension. The feeble efforts of the United States to publicize its policies abroad were going unheard.

But even with full recognition of the problem and its seriousness, there were several sizable hurdles to surmount. Not only was propaganda directed to foreign countries considered "unethical" and "meddling in the internal affairs" abroad, but propaganda itself was suspect. The public generally opposed propaganda since it generally implied underhanded tactics for ignoble ends. Congress feared propaganda in a somewhat different sense. Republicans even during the war had bitterly attacked the Office of War Information on the grounds that it might (some believed it would) be used to perpetuate the New Deal. For more than a decade Congress had followed a line of thought that all "propaganda" was "bad," but that legitimate "information" was all right. Hence, during the war, the Office of War Information was headed by Elmer Davis, a newsman, surrounded by a staff of expert reporters and journalists trained in "presenting the facts." In fact, as late as 1944, an official OWI report pridefully stated that its job was information, not propaganda, that it did not attempt to *persuade* anybody.

Even in the postwar information program abroad, information was the basic doctrine, uncolored and presumably unslanted toward any particular goal. When it came time to adopt a psychological warfare approach to meet Communist propaganda abroad, the change in emphasis was naturally a difficult one to achieve overnight. In fact, many observers still criticize current efforts on the grounds that sticking too closely to the truth is doing more harm than good abroad, that too much emphasis is still on information, not enough on propaganda.

BASIS FOR THE CAMPAIGN OF TRUTH [1]

The United States government is a relative newcomer in the field of international propaganda. As I use the term, and as the government conceives it, propaganda means simply a planned and organized effort to spread information and ideas through political or social entities. Our own expanded information program has been labeled by the President a "Campaign of Truth." It is indeed just that. Though I think I must admit . . . that in adopting this title we have rather made a virtue of necessity. Truth is the only commodity we can offer in this field, since in our free and democratic system duplicity of the type engaged in by our opponents would be quickly exposed. I suppose it is because of the association in our minds of the concepts of propaganda and duplicity as practiced by Hitler and Stalin, as well as

[1] From "The Voice of America: Spokesman of the Free World," by Foy D. Kohler, Chief, International Broadcasting Division, Department of State. *Proceedings of the Academy of Political Science.* 24:92-9. January 1951. Reprinted by permission.

a latent distrust of government activity in such a field, that we have been slow as a people to realize the importance of information—or, if you will, propaganda—as an instrument in the modern world.

STORY OF MODERN PROPAGANDA [2]

Webster's calls [propaganda] "any organized or concerted group effort, or movement to spread particular doctrines, information, etc." In this sense, propaganda is the influencing of people's ideas so that they will think or act in a certain manner. . . .

American history does not lack examples of propaganda in this broad sense. Many authors during the Revolution sought to unite public opinion behind the cause of independence, such as Thomas Paine who received from the Continental Congress in 1785 a resolution of thanks and a reward of $3,000 for his work, and his pamphlet *Common Sense* Washington found "is working a wonderful change in the minds of men." . . .

Following the First World War, however, the modern concept of organized, official propaganda developed, which came to have a stigma attached to it in the minds of most people. As the *Encyclopaedia Britannica* says, it "has come to be looked upon as mere advocacy of special interests or as an attempt to gain credence for statements partially or wholly untrue." Governments have conducted official propaganda campaigns to further public acceptance of their own policies.

A pioneer of propaganda in this modern concept was the English philosopher, Benjamin Kidd, who died in 1916. Noting the tremendous changes that had occurred in Japan, and in Germany under Bismarck, in the short space of two generations, he wrote: "It is clearly in evidence that the science of creating and transmitting public opinion under the influence of collective emotion is about to become the principal science of civilization to the mastery of which all governments and all powerful in-

[2] From "A Brief Story of Modern Propaganda," editorial. *Congressional Digest*. 27:43-4. February 1948. Reprinted by permission.

terests will in the future address themselves with every resource at their command."

Kidd's predictions gained strength during World War I. Before 1914 Germany alone among the great countries of the world carried on systematic propaganda. The Press Bureau of the German Foreign Office, affiliated bureaus and telegraphy agencies abroad, German embassies and legations, offices of foreign branches of German banks and shipping companies all did their best to spread impressions favorable to Germany, and to prevent as far as possible criticism of German foreign policy and internal affairs.

For some months after the war broke out the Germans had this field to themselves. . . . It was not until the spring of 1918 that the Allies fully felt the importance of the war of ideas. When the German military offensive of March had the Allied governments worried they decided to coordinate their respective propaganda facilities and engage in an all-out psychological attack on the enemy. The British and French each set up special departments of propaganda, and the United States spurred activities of the Creel Committee.

The impetus thus given to the war of words in World War I did not terminate with the Armistice in 1918. . . . From the very beginning of their regime the Bolsheviks heeded the advice of Marx that "physical force must be overthrown by physical force; but theory, too, becomes a physical force as soon as it takes possession of the masses." . . . Radio Moscow was first to broadcast in the principal languages of the world—political programs which, according to one authority, were "designed formerly to encourage world revolution, and more recently to win support in other countries for the foreign policy of Soviet Russia."

In Germany, ex-corporal Hitler early decided that his country had lost World War I because of the superiority of the Allies' psychological attack. The first political post he ever held, in the German Workers Party, was that of Chief of Propaganda. In 1923 he wrote his widely circulated book *Mein Kampf*, and after his release from prison rose to power with the aid of innumerable speeches, parades, songs, leaflets, newspapers, radio programs, etc. As a leader of the Third Reich, he appointed Goebbels as Minister of Propaganda. Goebbels, whose motto was "That propaganda is good which leads to success," in turn developed to a high pitch the technique of dividing, deceiving, confusing and weakening the will of those countries opposed to Germany's foreign policy by what is known as "terrorist propaganda." "Lord Haw-Haw" soon became a familiar figure to many in the English-speaking world. At the peak of this war of words it is estimated that the Germans spent more than a half a billion dollars annually for propaganda.

In Italy Mussolini, himself a former newspaperman, spared no effort in convincing the people of the soundness of his policies and affirming to the world that "the idea, doctrine and spirit of fascism are universal." . . .

On the other side of the world the Japanese adopted tactics familiar in certain occidental countries. Following the rise to power of the military faction in the early '30's they pictured repeatedly to their Asiatic neighbors the view that the white man must be expelled from Asia, and that Japan should be given leadership in what they termed the "Co-Prosperity Sphere." . . .

France and Great Britain started broadcasting to their colonies and dominions in 1931 and 1932, respectively. To strengthen her psychological defenses France soon added programs in German and Italian, but the British were slower in taking up the counter-offensive. Not until 1938 did they beam Arabic over the air waves to the Middle East, Spanish and Portuguese to Latin America, and—after Munich—German, French, and Italian to Europe.

Propaganda in the modern sense has developed through technological progress. With more people living in industrial centers, with more people working at similar jobs and having like interests, it is possible to present to greater numbers a single point of view. And in recent years communication facilities have greatly increased, such as daily newspapers, movies, and especially radios.

Of course citizens of the United States have taken advantage of these new means to promote their own particular interests. Many industrial leaders have recognized the value of public relations in the conduct of their business. Political parties use the press, radio, and movies to present their points of view, as do innumerable other organizations and individuals. But it is important to note that [until recently] the Federal Government itself [had] . . . never created a permanent body to systematically propagate information and ideas, either at home or abroad.

AMERICA'S ENTRANCE INTO THE PROPAGANDA FIELD [3]

Before [World War II] . . . international broadcasting was a private affair. The eleven transmitters in the United States were operated at a loss, primarily for prestige value. Some advertising was carried on the programs broadcast by these stations. But the programs were of an experimental type because the operators wanted to develop American "know-how" in international broadcasting.

In wartime, international broadcasting was part of our psychological warfare program and our propaganda activities. Now, probably basing its approval on the fact that the world was unsettled, Congress was willing to permit the State Department to inform other peoples of the earth, through an extensive and well thought out program, about America, her people and her aims. This program was extensive in the light of our past activities in the field, though not in terms of what other countries do. For instance, in middle 1942, Germany was reported to control sixty-eight transmitters and Japan, forty-six.

Even after the war began in 1939 the United States international information program developed slowly. In July 1941, Robert E. Sherwood was given the job of organizing the Foreign Information Service of the Office of Coordinator of Information. Regarding the situation at that time, he commented: "Although this nation was then building up its defenses, training an enormous army, there were no preparations being made for psychological warfare. Although the United States has led the world in

[3] From "Telling the World About America," by Dick Fitzpatrick, Managing Editor, *Newspaperman*, Washington, D.C. *Public Opinion Quarterly*. 10:582-92. Winter 1946. Reprinted by permission.

radio broadcasting, we had done little to develop international broadcasting from this continent."

On July 13, 1942, President Roosevelt issued an executive order consolidating informational activities of the government by establishing the Office of War Information. The director of the agency was instructed, among other things, to "formulate and carry out, through the use of press, radio, motion picture, and other facilities, information programs designed to facilitate the development of an informed and intelligent understanding, at home and abroad, of the status and progress of the war effort and of the war policies, activities, and aims of the government." The international information operations of this new agency were handled by its overseas branch which had Sherwood as its director.

To tell the world the American story during the war the government constructed nineteen international short-wave broadcast transmitters at a cost of $5,424,729. One of the transmitters was in operation before the OWI was created in June 1942. Four were put in operation in 1943, eleven were put in operation in 1944 and the last three began operation in January 1945.

Even before OWI had all its transmitters in operation, President Roosevelt was concerned with the need for continued direct international broadcasting after the war. On November 16, 1943, in a letter to the chairman of the Federal Communications Commission, he said, "If the principle of freedom to listen is to help in providing the basis for better understanding between the peoples of the world, it seems to me important that we lay the proper foundations now for an effective system of international broadcasting for the future years. . . . The problems as to the scope of the physical set-up and of the type of control to be exercised will become important."

However, in the government there was opposition to a program of direct international broadcasting. In 1944 the Interdepartment Radio Advisory Committee, which was established by the President, issued a report which said that the present system of international broadcasting was "unsound from an engineering standpoint." . . .

The government officials directly concerned with the program—Coordinator of Inter-American Affairs Nelson Rockefeller, who was responsible for the information activity in Latin America, and OWI Director Elmer Davis—came to the rescue of the program. Rockefeller said, "Short-wave broadcasting is an indispensable instrument for creating understanding of the United States," and "direct international short-wave broadcasting is the only medium that is not subject to foreign censorship or control." Davis declared, "It is generally held, I believe, that our national interest will be served by a much wider dissemination of American news throughout the world than was known before the war."

After much talk, on February 19, 1945, the State Department's special committee on communications approved a statement prepared by the Department which gave America's position on international broadcasting. The statement held that "direct short-wave broadcasts originating in the United States should be continued after the war on a daily basis," and "facilities, both as to quantity and quality, should in general be as good as those of any other country." When this statement of policy was issued the Interdepartment Radio Advisory Committee reversed its previous objection to international broadcasting. . . .

In the early summer of 1945, Dr. Arthur W. Macmahon of Columbia University, a consultant on administration to the State Department, prepared a "Memorandum on the Postwar International Information Program of the United States," which was made public six months later. . . . [Many of Dr. Macmahon's recommendations are now incorporated in the present information program. See first selection in section on "Current Strategy in the War of Ideas."—Ed.]

When the atom bomb finished Japan . . . President Truman won approval from newspaper and radio sources by abolishing the OWI on August 31, 1945. But in a statement issued when he signed the executive order abolishing the OWI and the Office of Inter-American Affairs, the President stated that "the nature of present day foreign relations makes it essential for the United States to maintain informational activities abroad as an integral part of the conduct of our foreign affairs." . . . Mr. Truman pointed out that . . . the overall task of the international information program is "to see to it that other peoples receive a full and fair picture of American life and of the aims and policies of the United States Government."

In the four months that followed, the foreign information activities of the OWI and OIAA—operating, as directed by the executive order, as the United States Interim Information Service—were consolidated.

On December 31, 1945, Secretary of State Byrnes wrote President Truman explaining the international information program that was to be put into effect the following day in a new organization called the Office of International Information and Cultural Affairs (OIC). It was to be headed by a director who would report to Assistant Secretary of State William Benton. Byrnes told the President that "there never was a time, even in the midst of war, when it was so necessary to replace prejudice with truth, distortion with balance, and suspicion with understanding."

The Secretary of State made two interesting points. (1) "Many countries," he said, "are interested in the development of this new medium (short-wave broadcasting) giving us direct access to the peoples of other lands who want to understand the American people and their policies," and (2) its use "will be a new departure for the United States, the last of the great nations of the earth to engage in informing other peoples about its policies and institutions." . . .

The most significant fact concerning the OIC's program is that it is a recognition by the President, by the State Department, and by the Congress that informational activities, particularly short-wave broadcasting, are actually essential and an integral part of the conducting of our foreign affairs. It is particularly striking that this type of activity has been approved in the United States where, traditionally, the idea of government engaging in informational activities is abhorrent and where the entrance of government into any new field is bitterly opposed.

The OIC program also is a recognition of the fact that in broadcasting to the peoples of the world, the American story must be a unified one. . . . Another important aspect of the program is that this government recognizes the importance to us of foreign public opinion.

OFFICE OF WAR INFORMATION [4]

"Psychological warfare," like "total war," is a phrase that has been given to us by our enemies. The reality behind both phrases is not new to Americans. Some of the techniques of psychological warfare require skills in which Americans have led the world. But one common concept of psychological warfare—that of a war of words in which men's loyalties and convictions are manipulated on a mass scale, and with controls which make falsehoods as effective as truths in influencing people—is an idea which belongs, at least in its modern formulation, to Hitler and Goebbels. And it can at least be argued that one of the significant Nazi achievements in psychological warfare has been their propagation of the phrase itself, and their conversion of many persons outside Germany to the belief that psychological warfare is some kind of technical magic done with mirrors.

Something like this belief forms the basis of one of the three charges most frequently brought against the overseas propaganda of the United States government. . . . The charge is that our propaganda work has been too simple, too provincially American, and too deeply committed to using truth as a weapon with which to confuse our enemies and give heart to our friends. . . .

It is certainly significant that . . . the word "information" has been used to describe the work. In Executive Order 9182, setting up the Office of War Information, the President recognized "the right of the American people and of all other peoples opposing the Axis aggressors to be truthfully informed about the war effort." He further instructed the Office of War Information to "formulate and carry out, through the use of press, radio, motion picture and other facilities, information programs designed to facilitate the development of an informed and intelligent understanding, at home and abroad, of the status and progress of the war effort and of the war policies, activities and aims of the government."

This assignment [did] . . . not rule out the techniques of "war of nerves." Many of these are recognized to be necessary

[4] From "Fighting with Information: OWI Overseas," by Joseph Barnes, Deputy Director, Atlantic operations, Office of War Information. *Public Opinion Quarterly.* 7:34-45. Spring 1943. Reprinted by permission.

in modern war against an enemy experienced in their use. But it [did] . . . rule out the technique of falsehood and much, if not all, of the strategy of terror. What this wording [did was] . . . to assign to the Office of War Information an overall job, on the long pull, of telling the truth.

Most Americans are prepared to admit today that the truth, in international communications, is something elastic. Most of them expect, for example, that this country's overseas propaganda will not concentrate in wartime on threats of strikes in airplane factories, or on ration difficulties, or on domestic political quarrels. They expect, instead an effective, intelligent presentation to the world of the strength of America, in men and resources, and they expect that if enough people abroad, both our friends and our enemies, are shown the truth about this country, it will shorten the war.

For better or worse, the Office of War Information . . . worked from the start to meet this expectation. There [were] . . . some factors beyond its control which by themselves might have forced its work to take this line. The United States is relatively far from the target areas of its propaganda, and selectivity of propaganda decreases with distance. Short-wave radio transmitters in this country, for example, include up to a dozen different countries in a single beam, and all evidence shows that European short-wave listening audiences are highly polylingual. This alone would make it difficult . . . to tell sharply contradictory stories to—say—the Hungarians and the Rumanians. Political warfare by adroit falsehood has been easier for the Nazis.

It was, however, not this problem of distance, nor the relative inexperience of Americans in European politics, nor the hunger of much of the foreign world for hard, cold news, nor any particular moral squeamishness which determined the Office of War Information to work out an American form of political warfare in which truth would be its chief weapon. It was, judging by the debates which the question . . . provoked for more than a year, rather the belief that a democratic society with a free press and a fighting belief in freedom could only weaken itself by adopting the patterns and the tricks or even the definition of Fascist psychological warfare.

A second postulate of the overseas work of the Office of War Information [was] . . . that it should concentrate on giving volume and tone and meaning to the Voice of America. . . .

So the Overseas Branch of the Office of War Information . . . tried to cash in on the imponderable assets of the Voice of America. Its most effective radio programs—those which . . . elicited most response in one form or another—used this phrase, followed by the phrase: "one of the United Nations." American short-wave transmitters [were] . . . put regularly at the service of the other United Nations. . . . But the information sent abroad directly by the Office of War Information, under its own name, [was] . . . consistently American in tone and approach.

Finally, there [was] . . . a third general directive under which the Office of War Information . . . worked out its overseas services. This [was] . . . the injunction, explicit and implicit, to all radio script or leaflet writers to stay carefully inside the limit of official United States foreign policy. To some critics, this . . . seemed an act of abdication in the field of psychological warfare. . . .

The Office of War Information . . . met this situation, probably, in the only ways it could. First, it . . . spread as widely as it could the speeches of United Nations leaders. . . . Second, it tried to match all talk of American power—"The United States does not lose wars"—with reiteration of American idealism and lack of aggressive motives—"The United States does not loot after its victories." Finally, it . . . concentrated on the long, daily, twenty-four hour grind of telling the world about the war, through every medium it could command. Regionalization of specialists and directives [was] . . . used to make certain that this telling of the truth [was] . . . in the words, and accents, and idioms of both speech and thought that are most intelligible to each separate foreign country.

AMERICA'S PROPAGANDA HURDLES [5]

American thinking on this subject [propaganda] since 1917 has shown a painful uncertainty. On the one hand, we wondered

[5] From "Propaganda and the Free Society," by Ralph Block, Special Assistant to the Director, Office of International Information, Department of State. *Public Opinion Quarterly*. 12:676-86. Winter 1948-49. Reprinted by permission.

whether it was correct for the United States Government in time of peace to try to influence foreign people by propaganda; and, on the other hand, whether it is proper for the government to use a powerful instrument that certainly was not mentioned in the Constitution. . . .

The United States Government established foreign propaganda as an avowed implement of foreign policy in both world wars; but the chief propagandists, George Creel and Elmer Davis, carried on under an astonishing load of odium. Then in 1948, after several false starts in 1946 and 1947, the Congress legally recognized propaganda (which was called information) as an instrument in the direction of foreign relations in behalf of the American society. In each case these affirmations have been attended by hesitation, and at no point have the executive departments and the Congress arrived at an agreed-upon definition of what they do or do not mean by propaganda. Playing over this 30-year history has been a belief, imbedded in democratic dogma, that factual truth or "information," as distinguished from "propaganda," produces a kind of self-acting transmutation in peoples abroad, leaving the initiator at a distance free to disclaim moral responsibility for "influencing" anyone.

In the democratic thesis, facts provide the basis for free judgment and decision; "propaganda" betrays the democratic principle. The latter has no essential preoccupation with truth; it is the guerrilla warfare of communication, it creeps up on your blind side saying one thing and meaning another; clothed in friendliness and good intentions like a bad fairy, it seduces you into taking a bite from the beautiful poisoned apple. In a world in which propaganda has increasingly overshadowed diplomacy as an instrument for influencing the course of international events, Americans remain uneasy in making concessions to its use, even as an instrument of defense. Indeed, it is possible that more Americans approve of the use of the atom bomb in defensive warfare than approve the use of propaganda to forestall war.

It may be inaccurate to attribute this reluctance entirely to the wellsprings of American moral ideas. In the deviation between public morality and its private counterpart . . . our libertarian tradition appears to be one thing and our practice is frequently another. . . . Nowhere else in the world are human beings so beset by oral and visual propaganda as Americans—by radio, newspapers, television, electric signs, billboards, and through the channels of the United States mail. Under the guise of advertising, propaganda is accepted as an integral factor in our social and economic pattern. . . .

Advertising appears to be generally accepted as an important function in the free market of the American economy. There is obviously a definable difference between the influence aimed at you as a consumer, which you can take or leave, and the influence which your government is aiming at foreign peoples in your behalf. . . . But in the United States the possibility that the inculcation of democratic virtues . . . might be propaganda never became acceptable doctrine; "education" and "information" were "good"; propaganda was always "bad."

In World War II, the United States Office of War Information ran head-on into a suspicion that it was an agent for propaganda to the American people. . . . Congressmen suspected OWI in its activities at home and abroad as a political instrument manipulated by a powerful President. Experts in foreign languages used in the psychological warfare branch were viewed with suspicion. In addition, there was the recurring mistrust of the kind of people engaged in propaganda, professional users of symbols—writers, journalists and artists—probably radicals, anyway not regular. . . .

Charles E. Bohlen, Counselor of the Department of State . . . in 1948 . . . made clear the distinction between "information" and "propaganda" from the standpoint of the United States Government:

> The integrity of our action and of the reputation of this government for honest dealing is one of the most priceless assets which the United States possesses. It cannot be bartered away for temporary propaganda advantage or even to offset temporary propaganda disadvantage.
>
> The deep-seated desire of the peoples of this earth for peace and tranquility cannot be regarded as expendable coin for propaganda purposes. . . .

To be alert to the danger of propaganda does not mean that we must ignore the vital necessity of clear public understanding of our policy purposes. That is quite a different matter.

Good publicity means accurate and continuous explanation and interpretation of our policy.

Propaganda means playing fast and loose with the truth as a means of confusing and not enlightening public opinion.

We cannot, and I am confident will not, permit our foreign policy to be at the mercy of foreign propaganda.

Among the other hurdles which must be cleared by a United States Government propagandist are the obviously different interpretations in a vigorous, developing society of the meaning of that society and of its constitutional sanctions. Who, for instance, can be trusted to find a mean common denominator of the virtues of American life which will permit every American to say, "Yes, that's us. You've hit the nail right on the head." The freedom to differ is the life blood of the American people; but how many Americans will agree, to take an easy instance, that *Oklahoma*, with its phenomenal long run in the American theater, would adequately interpret even one aspect of American life to foreign audiences. . . .

To those persons abroad who do not understand the mood in which the American people conduct their elections, the contradictions in the news must undoubtedly be confusing. . . . Even the most sophisticated foreigner seldom sees American events and institutions from the same perspective of understanding as Americans do. While we may cavil at the extravagance and distortion which appear in a considerable number of American motion pictures, we recognize these variations as representing . . . the Paul Bunyan spirit which is an inescapable factor in American entertainment. Foreigners as a rule take our movies, our comics, our sports, and all the other elements on the surface of our life as an accurate and literal index to our character. The problem of obtaining understanding abroad, therefore, is how to obtain it in terms of the frame of reference of those who observe us. Even the English, who speak the same approximate language, do not always arrive at an interpretation of us with which we would agree. . . . Facts can be as often misleading as not. . . .

Some aspects of American life may effectively interpret Americans to Europe and be without value in the Far East, and conversely. Few Americans moreover have a total picture of their country, as the chief propagandists must attempt to have. To do their work properly, propagandists must know that they are aiming at targets, and that the arrow must be different for each nation, and for each economic, political, and social level within foreign nations.

Is there any reason for the United States Government to engage in the projection of information about itself, its people, and its institutions except to influence other peoples in its favor and to help them to view American policies with understanding? The American people can demand that the promulgation of a propaganda program by their government be for purposes which are expressed openly and without deceit. But this assuredly is not to disallow that to influence foreign peoples in the interest of American ideals and policies is a justifiable interest of American statecraft.

It is a mistaken view of history to think that the responsibility of world leadership is something that has been thrust on our unwilling national brow. However reluctant we may be to leave our cozy national fireside for the alarums and excursions of the international open country, our whole history has been leading us step by step to this maturity. But if we are with due humility to live up to this responsibility, our propaganda cannot be merely an instrument of defense or offense. It must be transmuted by creative leadership into a vehicle of statesmanship. If this can be done, propaganda may be returned to its original meaning—the propagation of a faith, and propaganda will then be seen not in a narrow chauvinistic sense but as a means of continuing progress toward our ideal of the free dignity of man.

In this sense, American government propaganda in peace or in war must be guided by people who are clear about the essential meaning of American life. Not only the official propagandists but the legislators and administrators who sanction them must have an assured belief that the American scheme of living gives a satisfying explanation of the world today and will continue to provide a rationale by which the problems of tomorrow's world can be successfully resolved.

TODAY'S NEED FOR A CAMPAIGN OF TRUTH [6]

There has never been a time in our history when there was so great a need for our citizens to be informed and to understand what is happening in the world.

The cause of freedom is being challenged throughout the world today by the forces of imperialistic communism. This is a struggle, above all else, for the minds of men. Propaganda is one of the most powerful weapons the Communists have in this struggle. Deceit, distortion and lies are systematically used by them as a matter of deliberate policy. . . .

All too often the people who are subject to Communist propaganda do not know Americans, or citizens of the other free nations, as we really are. They do not know us as farmers or as workers. They do not know us as people having hopes and problems like their own. Our way of life is something strange to them. They do not even know what we mean when we say "democracy."

This presents one of the greatest tasks facing the free nations today. That task is nothing less than to meet false propaganda with truth all around the globe. Everywhere that the propaganda of Communist totalitarianism is spread, we must meet it and overcome it with honest information about freedom and democracy. . . .

The Communist propaganda portrays the Soviet Union as the world's foremost advocate of peace and the protector of defenseless peoples. The contradiction between what the Communist leaders have promised and what they have actually done is so startling that we are amazed that anyone can be deceived.

In Berlin, in Czechoslovakia, in the Balkans, in the Far East, they have proved, time after time, that their talk about peace

[6] From "Fight False Propaganda with Truth," by Harry S. Truman, President of the United States, an address before the American Society of Newspaper Editors, Washington, D.C., April 20, 1950. *Vital Speeches of the Day.* 16:442-4. May 1, 1950. Reprinted by permission.

is only a cloak for imperialism. But their intended victims will not learn these facts from Soviet propaganda. We are the ones who must make sure that the truth about communism is known everywhere.

At the same time, we must overcome the constant stream of slander and vilification that the Communists pour out in an effort to discredit the United States and other free nations.

Soviet propaganda constantly reviles the United States as a nation of "warmongers" and "imperialists." You and I know how absurd that is. We know that the United States is wholly dedicated to the cause of peace.

We have no purpose of going to war except in defense of freedom. Our actions demonstrate that we mean exactly what we say. But when men throughout the world are making their choice between communism and democracy, the important thing is not what we know about our purposes and our actions—the important thing is what they know. . . .

I am convinced that we should greatly extend and strengthen our efforts for making the truth known to people in all the world.

Most of us have recognized for years, of course, how important it is to spread the truth about freedom and democracy. We are already doing some very good work—through the Voice of America and the United States Information Offices and Libraries in many parts of the world, through the exchange of students, through the United Nations and its affiliated organizations, and in other ways.

But events have shown, I believe, that we need to do much more, both ourselves and in collaboration with the other free nations. We must use every means at our command, private as well as governmental, to get the truth to other peoples.

Private groups and organizations have an important part to play. Our labor unions have already done fine work in communicating with labor in Europe, in Latin America, and elsewhere. The story of free American labor, told by American trade unionists, is a better weapon against Communist propaganda among workers in other countries than any number of speeches by government officials. . . .

We should encourage many more people from other countries to visit us here, to see for themselves what is true and what is not true about our country.

We should find more opportunities for foreign students to study in our schools and universities. They will learn here the skills and techniques needed in their own countries. They will also see at first hand the rights and duties of citizens in our land of democratic institutions.

Our colleges should train more Americans to go abroad as teachers, especially to teach modern methods of farming, industry, and public health—and, by example, to teach our concepts of democracy. The notable record of our many charitable and religious organizations who send teachers abroad is proof of what can be done. . . .

The government's programs for telling the truth about the United States to the peoples of the world also need constant improvement. Our present overseas information and educational exchange program is getting results. For example, the Voice of America has been carrying to people behind the Iron Curtain the true story of world events. . . .

Because of the pressing need to increase our efforts along this line, I have directed the Secretary of State to plan a strengthened and more effective national effort to use the great power of truth in working for peace. This effort will require the imagination and energies of private individuals and groups throughout the country. We shall need to use fully all the private and governmental means that have proved successful so far—and to discover and employ new ones.

Our task is to present the truth to the millions of people who are uninformed or misinformed or unconvinced. Our task is to reach them in their daily lives, as they work and learn. We must be alert, ingenious, and diligent in reaching people of other countries, whatever their educational and cultural backgrounds may be. Our task is to show them that freedom is the way to economic and social advancement, the way to political independence, the way to strength, happiness, and peace.

This task is not separate and distinct from other elements of our foreign policy. It is a necessary part of all we are doing to build a peaceful world. It is as important as armed strength or economic aid. The Marshall Plan, military aid, Point Four—these and other programs depend for their success on the understanding and support of our own citizens and those of other countries.

We must make ourselves known as we really are—not as Communist propaganda pictures us. We must pool our efforts with those of the other free peoples in a sustained, intensified program to promote the cause of freedom against the propaganda of slavery. We must make ourselves heard round the world in a great campaign of truth.

We have tremendous advantages in the struggle for men's minds and loyalties. We have truth and freedom on our side. The appeal of free institutions and self-government springs from the deepest and noblest aspirations of mankind. It is based on every man's desire for liberty and opportunity. It is based on every man's wish to be self-reliant and to shape his own destiny.

As we go forward with our campaign of truth, we will make lasting progress toward the kind of world we seek—a world in which men and nations live not as enemies but as brothers.

THE STEPPED-UP TRUTH OFFENSIVE [7]

The principal propaganda weapon in the ideological battle with communism has been the Voice of America. Foreign information activities, including the Voice of America, were conducted during the war by the overseas branch of the Office of War Information and transferred to the State Department immediately after cessation of hostilities. Opposition in Congress to government broadcasting in peacetime led to repeated clashes over appropriations for the purpose and kept the program on a year-to-year basis until 1948, when the Information and Educational Exchange (Smith-Mundt) Act finally gave statutory backing to worldwide radio and other government international information and cultural activities. Since then, appropriations for those activities have steadily mounted.

[7] From "Non-Military Weapons in Cold-War Offensive," by Buel W. Patch, senior member of research staff, *Editorial Research Reports.* 1:259-67. April 12, 1951. Reprinted by permission.

In an address before the American Society of Newspaper Editors on April 20, 1950, two months before the start of Communist aggression in Korea, President Truman announced that he had directed the Secretary of State "to plan a strengthened and more effective national effort to use the great power of truth in working for peace." He declared that this task was not distinct from other elements of foreign policy but was "a necessary part of all we are doing to build a peaceful world."

In mid-July, when Communist propaganda was trying to make the world believe that the United States was the aggressor in Korea, President Truman asked Congress to implement his call for "a great campaign of truth" by granting a supplemental appropriation of $89 million for foreign information activities in the fiscal year 1951. In the end, Congress made available in regular and supplemental appropriations a total of only $94 million, but that sum was twice the amount appropriated for fiscal 1950.

After making a budget request for $115 million for fiscal 1952, the President on March 5 sought a supplemental $97.5 million to be made immediately available to speed up construction of additional radio facilities originally scheduled for completion over the next two years. On April 9, however, the House accepted a committee proposal to slash the proposed supplemental amount to only $9.5 million. Although expressing its belief that "properly managed and directed, the Voice of America is the best medium for . . . a campaign of truth," the committee said it was "very much disappointed with the accomplishments and progress made to date." Some $40 million of the $115 million requested in regular appropriations for foreign information activities in fiscal 1952 is earmarked for the Voice of America.

[Budget estimates for foreign information activities in fiscal 1952 assigned $25 million to radio program operations and $15.8 million to establishment of radio facilities. The amount for program operations is more than twice the estimate of $12 million for that account in fiscal 1951.—Ed.]

The 1951 appropriation included funds for a new program to increase the size of the audience by furnishing radio receivers to individuals in certain foreign countries. . . . The Smith-Mundt

Act authorized only dissemination of information about the United States. That limitation has not been so narrowly interpreted, however, as to prevent occasional resort to devices in the nature of psychological warfare or to prevent constant efforts "to encourage the sort of quiet doubts, foot-dragging, and passive resistance that the situation so clearly justifies." In fact, Assistant Secretary of State Barrett has defined the four chief objectives as:

1. Exposing to the world, directly and indirectly, the truly reactionary, vicious, and phony nature of Kremlin communism.

2. Building up a spirit of unity, spunk, determination, and confidence in all the nations of the free world.

3. Inculcating in other peoples a readiness and desire to cooperate with America—by disproving Soviet lies about us and by making clear that we are a resolute, strong, and honest nation whose moral strength and physical strength can be counted on.

4. Building, behind the Iron Curtain, psychological obstacles to further Kremlin aggression.

Barrett has opposed using methods of the "skywriting school of propaganda" or "blatant and blaring techniques," which he fears would "create the adverse impression of trying to buy the minds of men with American dollars." And he said, December 4, that "if, as some demand, we try to incite citizens in slave areas to open resistance at this time, we will merely be inviting our friends to commit suicide." On the radio, March 15, Senator Mundt (R., S.D.) said he thought the job, as to Russia, was primarily "to drive a wedge of suspicion between the ordinary Russian . . . and the government gauleiter," and that "so long as we're not in a shooting war . . . we should continue to tell the truth." . . .

General Marshall told a Senate Foreign Relations subcommittee last July 5 that the "guiding principle" must always be the truth and that it "would be most dangerous if we got into the kind of propaganda that is sometimes thought of." At the same time, he asserted that a more dynamic program was needed to meet the Soviet propaganda attack. Twenty-eight senators, writing a joint letter to President Truman on August 18, 1950, urged "a psychological and spiritual offensive against the Kremlin."

Referring to the Voice of America, the senators asserted that "more than money, we need a new vigor, a new imagination, a new directness and plainness of speech." Both Senator Benton (D., Conn.), who served as Assistant Secretary of State in charge of foreign information activities from 1945 to 1947, and Senator Mundt have offered measures calling for broad inquiries into existing programs and operations and means of making them more effective.

THE MEANINGS OF PSYCHOLOGICAL WARFARE [8]

Of psychological warfare one can . . . say that it is neither psychology nor war. The term covers a field of activity in the realm of politics, foreign affairs, communications, publicity and propaganda. In essence, it means the use of all available media of communications for the purpose of destroying the enemy's will to fight.

Modern psychological warfare is more inclusive than old-fashioned propaganda in its sphere of operations, and less naive in its faith in the efficacy of one-sidedness and calculated falsehood. It tends to place some confidence in the teachings of the sciences of man, notably social psychology and cultural anthropology. It tries to understand the audience and acts on the assumption that words alone do not win wars or campaigns. To be effective, words must be coupled with action. Hence psychological warfare is closely tied to political or military policy.

In the United States, as elsewhere, psychological warfare is a part of foreign policy. Most of its activities are centered in the State Department under an Assistant Secretary of State for Public Affairs. At present its annual budget is $79 million. The armed forces have their own psychological warfare branches, usually for tactical combat purposes in battle.

Psychological warfare, about which we are going to hear more and more as the cold war intensifies (and still more if and

[8] From "Psychological Warfare and Foreign Policy," by Saul K. Padover, Professor of Politics and History in the Graduate Faculty and Dean of the School of Politics in the New School for Social Research; formerly Psychological Warfare officer, AUS. *American Scholar*. 20, no2:151-61. [April] 1951. Copyright, 1951, by United Chapters of Phi Beta Kappa. Reprinted by permission.

when general shooting begins), is not merely an exercise of the vocal chords or the printing press. . . . World War II, when the phrase "psychological warfare" became current, saw two new developments. One was the use of loud-speakers and other devices, such as leaflet bombs, on the field of battle, in order to induce the enemy to surrender. The other was the large-scale and systematic application of radio to political warfare. In terms of the history of war, this young medium of communication which can encircle the earth and cross all man-made borders was as much of a new weapon as the atomic bomb. Today this "whispering gallery," as Woodrow Wilson described radio, is the main instrument of ideological warfare and propaganda. It is aimed essentially at civilian audiences over the face of the earth.

Both the Americans and Russians are fully engaged at present in the battle of the vocal chords. Sound is reinforced by print and picture. It is a war to which the average, even reasonably well-informed American has paid too little attention. Yet in its implications and repercussions, the psychological warfare now being waged may be at least as important as the fighting in Korea.

No one is more keenly aware of the value of political propaganda than are the Communist Russians. They know that underlying the diplomatic-political-military aspects of the global cold war, is the ideological struggle, the conflict for human loyalties and beliefs. They are alert to the possibilities of using human emotions, hopes and fears and aspirations, as prime political ammunition. They give the impression of being convinced that, in the end, the struggle between the East and West will not be won so much on the field of battle as in the hearts and minds of men.

The Soviet Union's propaganda machine, for use both at home and abroad, is one of the most formidable instruments for the shaping of beliefs in the world today. It employs hundreds of thousands of professionals at home. Abroad it has fervent and devoted allies who repeat the Soviet arguments and carry out its policies. When one keeps in mind that there are more than twenty million Communist party members outside the Soviet Union, not to mention the tens of millions of their fellow-travelers, one begins to realize what an immense pro-Russian propaganda force exists. Everywhere and at all times these people propagate the line laid down by the Kremlin. They may, indeed, be regarded as the Soviet Union's powerful foreign legion in psychological warfare.

What do they say in their propaganda? As is well known, the United States has become Moscow's chief devil. Against America, Soviet propaganda follows three main themes:

1. United States is corrupt, run by Big Business.
2. United States is imperialist, determined to dominate the world economically.
3. United States is a warmonger, out to destroy "the people's democracies."

The Communists' anti-American propaganda is not mere hate or willfulness or words spoken out of ignorance. On the contrary, it is a long-range strategic offensive against the free world; it is part of the far-reaching policy of undermining the United States even before a single bullet is fired, and thereby substantially weakening the one power capable of resisting or blocking Communist imperialism. In other words, the Kremlin propaganda line is not a conventional name-calling affair, but an integral instrument of total aggression on a global scale.

Consider, for example, the theme that the United States is a warmonger. Propaganda-wise, nothing could be more clever. As a smoke screen, it enables communism to cloak its planned aggressions as a supposed defense against so-called American warmongering machinations. Thus in the case of Korea, the Soviet and Chinese line has been that imperialist Americans with the aid of South Koreans invaded the innocent "people's democracy" of North Korea. This is the well-known technique of the Big Lie. As George Orwell put it, in the Communist language night is day, black is white, war is peace, brutality is love. This particular Big Lie about United States aggression is of particular importance with regard to the future, for it is a strategic maneuver intended to destroy either America's will to action or its moral ground before action. Should, for example, Communist aggressions and provocations become so intolerable as to move the United States to take armed steps, the Russian will be in a position to announce to the world a triumphant, "I told you so."

How does the United States counter this world-wide offensive? For a long time the American people and Congress failed to appreciate fully the extent of the Communist ideological penetration. Congress was suspicious, if not openly contemptuous, of anything that smacked of "propaganda," and the general public was not sufficiently informed of its significance in this age of mass communications. Thus, as soon as World War II was over, wartime agencies like OWI and OSS, with their skilled and experienced personnel, were disbanded, and a limited number of their functions were transferred to the State Department. The ablest individuals in the field left government service, and their loss has been tragic and irreplaceable. As a result of such shortsightedness, the United States all but lost the first round of the cold war to the Communists in Europe (even in Western Europe) and in Asia.

It was not until 1948 that Congress took some steps to catch up with the Russians. On January 27, 1948, it passed the Smith-Mundt Act "to promote a better understanding of the United States in other countries, and to increase mutual understanding between the people of the United States and the people of other countries." Under the Act, a number of information and propaganda agencies were set up in the State Department, the most important among them being the Office of Educational Exchange (OEX) and the Office of International Information (OII). . . .

One must emphasize that psychological warfare in itself is not a policy, but an instrument. These are things it cannot do. It cannot, in the long run, get away with systematic falsehoods. It cannot impose an alien system of values on one that already exists. It cannot alter basic institutions or satisfy physical needs or permanently substitute words for deeds.

But properly used—which means always in coordination with action—it can encourage friends and discourage enemies. It can undermine and disrupt. It can neutralize the potentially hostile or wavering. Tied to military action, it can help to confuse the enemy, damage his morale, put him on the defensive. In wartime, for example, it can make systematic appeals to the latent nationalisms in the Soviet orbit and stimulate discontent that would lead to disruptive action. . . .

All world-political signs indicate that we are in for a long conflict on ideological grounds, and one that will continue whether there is general shooting or not. In fact, it would be wise to act on the assumption that even if a general war should break out and should end in an American military victory, there will be a prolonged political aftermath of global proportions. Postwar upheavals all over the earth will require the ablest, the steadiest, the most skilled and sophisticated American political guidance—if this country is to survive as a world power.

THE WEAPONS AND ORGANIZATION OF PSYCHOLOGICAL WARFARE

EDITOR'S INTRODUCTION

Since the objective of psychological warfare is to *persuade,* whether the persuasion is to create a favorable response or to create fear, the weapons of psychological warfare are many. Any means of communicating ideas is a potential weapon of sykewar.[1] Hitler preferred direct communication via the spoken word and used to boast that "give him three hours and he'd have any audience eating out of his hand." While his main preference was for mass meetings lasting for hours in which he could play upon the emotions of his audience directly with the aid of carefully planned effects (flags, drums, stage lighting, rehearsed "Sieg Heils," etc.), all the stadia in Germany were inadequate to reach all the German people. So he turned to radio as the most effective second choice in dissemination of the spoken word. And it was upon radio that he depended primarily in his bloodless "terror" campaigns against Austria, the Rhineland, Czechoslovakia and Poland. The Nazi technique provided the basis for sykewar practiced by the rest of the world in World War II.

During the war, however, reaching an "enemy" population directly was almost impossible via the spoken word. Radio broadcasting was relegated to a position of secondary importance by all of the belligerents, and chief reliance was placed by the military upon leaflet propaganda of many types.

And in the experience of most of the sykewar professionals serving the United States during World War II, these were practically the only weapons of psychological warfare—radio broadcasting and printed material (leaflets dropped over enemy territory by plane, fired in leaflet shells, or distributed by the "underground" in occupied countries).

But the weapons of psychological warfare include any and all means of communicating ideas. Radio and the printed page naturally head the list, as far as the mass communications media are concerned. But cartoons, posters, slogans, exhibits, fairs, motion pictures, and scores of others must be included. Educational, cultural and technical exchange of persons has become a major weapon in the American sykewar arsenal. So has advertising by American firms trading abroad, release of American patents, the ECA, wheat for India, and a long list of other examples of words and deeds calculated to create goodwill for America abroad.

[1] "Sykewar" is a term "borrowed" from Daniel Lerner's book by that name. Lerner, Chief Editor, Intelligence Branch, Psychological Warfare Division, Supreme Headquarters AEF, during the war, coined the term to simplify reference to psychological warfare.

The organization of the stepped-up sykewar campaign on the part of the United States may be classified under two headings: the official program administered by the State Department under the terms of the Smith-Mundt Act of 1948, and private efforts usually instigated by and with the collaboration of the State Department. The main effort, of course, is that of the State Department itself, which not only has its own agencies for psychological warfare, but acts as general coordinator for the information activities of more than a score of other government agencies and bureaus dealing in the international sphere.

Since the complete program includes hundreds of smaller operations in a large number of different areas, involving scores of councils, committees and liaison officers, only the more important organizational aspects of American sykewar will be included here—chiefly those provided for specifically by the Smith-Mundt Act itself.

THE OFFICE OF INTERNATIONAL INFORMATION (OII) [2]

The Eighty-first Congress voted $79 million to provide for the intensification of our efforts to reach people in critical areas of the world through greatly strengthened medium-wave and short-wave broadcasts and through expanded programs for the exchange of persons, press and publications, libraries and institutes, and motion pictures.

The whole program calls for more than $63 million in appropriations and authorization to use $15 million in foreign currencies from ECA counterpart funds. Approximately $41 million will be used to establish six powerful transmittters for the Voice of America programs. The remaining $38 million is to take care of stepped-up radio and other media operations in 28 selected countries. Such increased activity includes the initiation of new language programs for the Voice of America; more publications, increased press services; a larger quantity and greater diversity of books, motion pictures, posters, exhibits and other visual materials. . . .

This program is carried out overseas through approximately 150 United States Information Service offices, which seek to sup-

[2] From "International Information Program of United States Department of State: The Campaign of Truth," a 7-page mimeographed release by the Department in 1950.

plement the normal processes of diplomacy by establishing contacts with government officials, newspaper editors and writers, professional groups, and leaders in various other fields. In all countries, the USIS works in close cooperation with United States diplomatic and consular missions.

Under the jurisdiction of the Assistant Secretary of State for Public Affairs, the Office of International Information (OII) is charged with coordinating and executing the international information program through three media divisions: Division of International Press and Publications; Division of International Broadcasting; Division of International Motion Pictures.

THE INTERNATIONAL BROADCASTING DIVISION (IBD—"THE VOICE OF AMERICA") [3]

Program Operations Branch: The Program Operations Branch comprises three basic services. They are the News Section, the Language Sections, and the Production Section.

The News Section prepares a daily basic news file gathered from the news services at the disposal of the International Broadcasting Division for translation and adaptation by the Language Units. It supplements this news file with analyses and interpretations of the news, talks, editorial roundups from the press of the nation, features on a variety of subjects, and dramatic presentations for translation and adaptation by the Language Units.

The Language Units are organized in six sections, namely, Slavic and Balkan, Western and Northern Europe, Far Eastern, Near and Mid-Eastern, Latin American, and English. They prepare for daily broadcasts radio scripts consisting of news, commentaries and features. Each Unit translates and adapts material from the basic news file, commentaries, and features prepared by the News Section. In addition, each originates commentary and feature material of a highly specialized and regional nature. Besides these Language Units, an English Section prepares radio scripts consisting of news, commentary, and features for broadcasts to the world in English.

[3] From *The World Audience for the Voice of America,* Office of International Information and Educational Exchange, Department of State, May 1, 1950. p2-9.

IBD currently broadcasts a total of 28¾ hours daily, of which 9 hours are in English to all areas and 19¾ hours are in the following languages; many of the originations are rebroadcast at certain times in various parts of the world, and Russian can be heard 24 hours a day:

30 minutes Arabic
45 minutes German to Austria
45 minutes Bulgarian
30 minutes Cantonese
60 minutes Czech/Slovak
45 minutes French
45 minutes German to Germany
30 minutes Greek
45 minutes Hungarian
15 minutes Indonesian
70 minutes Italian
45 minutes Korean
90 minutes Mandarin
30 minutes Persian
60 minutes Polish
30 minutes Portuguese
30 minutes Rumanian
150 minutes Russian
45 minutes Serbo-Croat
15 minutes Slovene
30 minutes Spanish to Spain
140 minutes Spanish to Latin America
30 minutes Turkish
30 minutes Ukrainian

The Production Section supplies the directors, narrators, announcers, actors, and music for the actual broadcasts. In performing its function, the Production Section is responsible for the application of the most effective radio production techniques in broadcasting the scripts prepared by the Language Units. The Special Events Unit of this Section provides to Language Units on-the-spot interviews with prominent personalities, forums and talks by specialists in various fields, and coverage of outstanding events throughout the United States and various parts of the world.

The Overseas Distribution Unit . . . supplements the actual broadcasting prepared by the Program Operations Branch by providing recordings, together with the scripts and/or program notes, to USIS offices in Europe, Latin America, the Near and Middle East, and the Far East (a total of 98 distribution points) for rebroadcast on medium wave by foreign stations. This service consists of recording IBD original broadcasts and domestic network broadcasts, as well as special programs prepared specifically for distribution overseas. Peak distribution has reached 13,000 discs in one month. This service extends the scope of the OII informational program by making it possible to reach a wider audience than may be reached through direct broadcasts.

For example, to Singapore, Malaya, 40 music transcriptions are sent monthly together with program notes, and, in addition, English programs such as Hit-Parade, University Theater, Cavalcade of America, Martin Block Make Believe Ballroom, and Chinese (Mandarin) feature and music programs, totaling 62 transcriptions monthly. The American Embassy reports air time upwards of 34 hours monthly on Radio Malaya devoted to these recordings. Additional special programs are furnished from time to time, as well as scripts for local production on various topics such as developments in medicine, science, literature, child care, public health, etc. . . .

The programming to the various areas varies as to content in accordance with local political conditions and interests, as well as the availability or lack thereof of a free flow of information in each country. Thus, to Eastern Europe, the Voice of America broadcasts preponderantly news, and commentaries of a political and economic type; whereas, to Western Europe, cultural information and feature presentations make up a larger proportion of the output; to the Near and Mid-East, agricultural and information features as well as music and poetry make up the greater part of the programs; to the Far East, news and political analyses form the major share of each broadcast; to Latin America, features and a lighter type of programming are presented.

The Voice of America broadcasts emanating in New York are relayed or rebroadcast in Europe by the following services: The British Broadcasting Corporation, the American Relay Base in Europe (Munich), Radio Salonika, Radiodiffusion Française (France), Radio in American Sector (Berlin), German Stations in U. S. Zone (Germany), Rot-Weiss-Rot (Austrian Radio Network), Radio Audizioni Italia—Italian Radio Network, Greek Local Stations, and, in North Africa by Tangier.

In the Far East they are relayed or rebroadcast by Honolulu and Manila, Radio Hongkong, and the Korean Broadcasting System; in the Near East by Radio Tehran; and in Latin America by approximately 30 independent stations in various Latin American countries.

Facilities Branch: The Facilities Branch comprises four sections: the Network Operations Section, the Engineering Section, the Operations Section, and the Relay Bases Section. The Network Operations Section provides for the physical formation and operation of the network and short-wave transmitters. [It] organizes, plans, and allocates the use of wire-line facilities and internal studio and recording facilities. The Engineering Section develops the requirements for technical facilities in the United States and abroad to meet the needs of future broadcasting, construction, and maintenance. [It makes] propagation studies and recommendations. The Operations Section is responsible for the operation of studio, recording and transmission facilities in accordance with schedules prepared by the Network Operations Section. The Relay Bases Section is responsible for direction of operation at Honolulu and, in collaboration with the Foreign Service, direct operation of other relay bases. . . .

Program Evaluation Branch: The Program Evaluation Branch is comprised of three sections: the Analysis Section, the Audience Mail Section, and the Program Information Section.

The function of the Analysis Section is to evaluate the effectiveness of the worldwide output of the Voice of America. More specifically, the Analysis Section has the following main objectives: (a) To provide a well-rounded and objective picture of the VOA output. (b) To measure the size and characteristics of the VOA audience all over the world. (c) To determine which parts of the respective VOA programs are most effective and to what extent the stated objectives of the VOA [are] accomplished. (d) To make some estimate of the competitive position of the VOA. (e) To recommend policy and program changes on the basis of these findings and to test the effects of such changes.

To attain these objectives, the Analysis Section sponsors large-scale research projects in the field, carried out by recognized private and academic research organizations. Currently under way are contracted studies of audience size, distribution and characteristics in four European countries, program evaluation studies in five European and three Latin American countries, content analyses studies of press and radio reaction to the VOA in Iron Curtain countries, comparative analyses of VOA, BBC and USSR output to Germany, and a systematic content analysis of VOA scripts at specified time intervals.

In addition, the staff of the Analysis Section carries on continuing research projects. These include reports on coverage of the VOA as indicated by audience mail, weekly reports on Iron Curtain reactions to the VOA, statistical reports on the worldwide distribution of receiver sets, peak listening hours and the like, content analyses of audience mail by language, and monthly evaluation of VOA effectiveness by area, based on field reports and intelligence material.

The Audience Mail Section handles and processes approximately 130,000 letters annually, addressed to the Voice of America, from the far corners of the world. It acknowledges audience mail in the language of the original letter, supplies as far as possible all information requested herein, and prepares quantitative reports on audience mail for use by IBD and other offices of the Department.

From July 1, 1949, to March 31, 1950, the Program Information Section printed and distributed to listeners, by direct mail and by local dissemination through United States overseas field missions, four bi-monthly issues of the Voice of America radio program schedules.

The schedules have a multiple purpose: to keep listeners informed of the times, titles and frequencies of programs; to serve as a medium for evaluating listenership as evidenced by audience response to broadcast offers of the schedule; and finally, by stimulating a continuing flow of listener mail, to provide direct audience reaction to Voice of America broadcasts.

The four issues . . . were published in eight languages. . . . Each language edition is distributed to a worldwide audience, i.e., the French schedule is mailed in response to specific requests from French-speaking listeners in France and in approximately a hundred other areas of the world, etc. From July 1, 1949, to March 31, 1950, [more than two million] . . . copies of the schedule were disseminated to listeners by direct mail or by United States overseas field missions with distribution by language editions as follows:

English	324,983
Far East	19,291
French	251,128
German	538,375
Italian	186,220
Spanish (Spain)	64,768
Portuguese	216,729
Spanish (L.A.)	511,014

The Program Information Section also supplies, upon request, stories and photos on the Voice of America staff and operations for promotion in foreign radio magazines and newspapers.

THE INTERNATIONAL PRESS AND PUBLICATIONS DIVISION (INP) [4]

A constant flow of documentary press, feature, and pictorial material about United States Government actions, policies, and many phases of American life is produced for publication overseas by the International Press and Publications Division.

This information is distributed through United States Information Service offices abroad to an estimated 10,000 foreign newspapers and periodicals, reaching more than 90,000,000 readers throughout the world. Approximately 75,000 foreign government officials, editors, and other leaders of public opinion receive INP materials. To deliver this information to all parts of the world, INP maintains a number of regular services. These may be grouped into four broad categories—fast-moving or news material; feature products; visual material; and publications.

[4] From "International Information Program of United States Department of State: The Campaign of Truth," a 7-page mimeographed release by the Department in 1950. p4-5.

Principal product in the fast-moving news category is the *Wireless Bulletin*, with five editions daily, six days a week: the *European Bulletin,* the *Night Bulletin,* the *Middle and Near East Bulletin,* the *Latin American Bulletin,* and the *Far East Bulletin.* Each bulletin is transmitted by Morse or radioteletype and runs approximately 7,000 words. The *Bulletin* is monitored by 60 United States diplomatic missions and from these points airmailed to other missions not having reception facilities. United States Information Service offices distribute the *Bulletin* to American and foreign press agencies, to newspapers, foreign government officials, United States foreign service personnel, and other interested groups and persons.

Feature material offers an effective way of portraying to other countries facts about the United States Government, and the American people—their cultural, social, and economic progress. Such material, in various forms, is distributed to foreign newspapers, magazines, and radio stations. It includes a 10-page *Air Bulletin,* issued twice a week and airmailed to all United States missions; special feature articles; regular columns; and reprints of magazine articles designed to counteract adverse foreign propaganda as well as to depict life in the United States.

INP also produces, in cooperation with leading professional associations, five scientific newsletters (medical, surgical, dental, chemical, and pharmaceutical). These are distributed overseas to doctors, scientists, universities, health groups, and foreign scientific journals. Since mid-1948, INP has been publishing these technical newsletters in English, French, and Spanish.

Magazines and pamphlets provide basic information about the United States, its institutions, and way of life. Among the magazines produced and distributed by INP is *Amerika,* an illustrated monthly nonpolitical Russian-language magazine, averaging 75 pages. Approximately 50,000 copies of each issue are sent to Russia for distribution by a Soviet news agency. Material for three German-language magazines published in Germany is prepared and edited in New York. The production of a magazine for Korea was discontinued on the outbreak of hostilities but will be resumed with the restoration of peace in that country.

Pamphlets providing compact, basic information about the United States have been in great demand in foreign schools and in adult education groups. A grand total of more than 3,000,000 copies of pamphlets have been produced by or for INP in the past few years. For example, 620,000 copies of "An Outline of American History" were distributed in 10 languages. "A Government by the People" was translated into 19 languages and "Toward World Peace and Progress," a 16-page description of the fundamental objectives of American foreign policy, into 20 languages.

"Sinews of America," an illustrated booklet dealing with America's material strength, was translated into 24 languages, with 508,000 copies distributed.

THE INTERNATIONAL MOTION PICTURES DIVISION (IMP) [5]

This division comprises two branches—Film Operations Branch with three sections as follows: Utilization Section, Program and Liaison Section, and Overseas Distribution Section, in Washington; and Production Branch with four sections as follows: Adaptation and Technical Services Section, Foreign Versions Section, Private Industry Liaison Section, and Administrative and Services Section, in New York.

IMP initiates, plans, and develops motion-picture projects depicting various phases of life in the United States. It cooperates with other federal agencies and nongovernmental agencies and organizations in planning and developing programs which involve official use of motion pictures abroad and in shaping such programs to fit the requirements of specific areas and activities.

In performing these functions the division procures, adapts, edits, contracts for production, and rescores film materials in selected languages for use in the program. It acquires prints of approved productions and equipment necessary for presenting the

[5] From *The World Audience for America's Story.* Department of State Publication 3485 (International Information and Cultural Series 5), April 1949. p79-82.

program and distributes such equipment and materials for use abroad.

It analyzes and evaluates reports from United States Foreign Service establishments concerning the effectiveness of the international motion-picture program, using these as guides in planning the division's activities.

It should be noted that, in fiscal year 1947, 39 privately owned and produced subjects were acquired and adapted for the program, and 33 subjects were produced under private contract. These acquired and produced films were recorded in some or all of 26 languages, and a total of 2,011 language-version reels were prepared during the year. Over 28,000 print reels were distributed to more than 200 overseas film libraries.

In fiscal year 1948, available funds were adequate only for the completion of English versions then in process. No foreign-language versions were recorded, and few prints were dispatched to the field.

In 1949 . . . the program . . . included 50 subjects totaling 100 reels . . . , 30 subjects acquired from outside sources, and 20 . . . produced under private contract . . . and a total of 20,000 print reels . . . sent abroad. [Ed. note: Films are currently produced in 29 languages, each film being made up in approximately 15 language versions. About 300 prints of each title are distributed in the field.]

Method of Distribution. The division distributes the films through the 73 foreign service establishments listed, and these, in turn, distribute to posts under their jurisdiction. The films are made available free of charge to business, professional, and scientific groups, religious groups, community-service organizations, hospitals and educational institutions, government groups, workers' groups, etc. The theatrical exhibition of selected USIS films is accomplished in certain areas through the cooperation of American distribution companies, as in the Netherlands, for example. Of course, the nontheatrical distribution and exhibition is handled through the USIS staffs.

Selection of Films. Sample prints of existing films which may meet the requirements of the program are obtained from governmental and private sources. . . . Those tentatively selected are then discussed with country specialists and other officers of the department for approval as to suitability, suggestions regarding editing, the preparation of new commentaries, and other necessary changes. Often owners of acquired films allow their productions to be used without charge; however, the department frequently must pay the costs of re-editing, preparation of foreign language versions, and printing. (Examples: "Guarding Health in Rural Schools," a portrayal of small rural schools' ways of education for prevention, in addition to proper care and treatment, of minor ills; "Clean Waters," showing the problem of waste disposal and how it is solved in American communities of various sizes. . . .)

Films of the above type play a very important role in the program, particularly in the professional fields. However, they cannot fill the special needs for pictures showing representative phases of American life in terms understandable to foreign audiences. To obtain these films the department contracts for their production by private documentary film producers with guidance from the department. (Examples: "The Doctor," a portrayal of the community as its physical ills are treated by a general practitioner who also serves on the Board of Education; "The County Agent," a story which not only demonstrates the position and functions of his activities but shows a number of Americans working together to solve their problems. . . .)

Specialized Technical Films. Members of most of the professions are interested to know what their colleagues in the United States are doing and find the motion picture an invaluable tool for learning of American experiments and techniques. In response to the demand for such films limited quantities of prints of various titles have been sent to a number of posts. The subjects covered are medicine, surgery, dentistry and dental surgery, psychology, and physiotherapy, as well as engineering subjects and samples of teaching films for study by educationists. . . .

There are over 700 16mm projectors being used by USIS in the field, supplied by the Motion Pictures Division. These are made available to schools, organizations, institutions, etc., for the exhibition of USIS films. Several local USIS offices hold instruction classes on the use of motion-picture equipment. The Motion Pictures Division must provide and maintain projectors, screens, electrical accessories, motor generator units, transformers, etc., and in many countries special mobile units for reaching provincial audiences.

The mobile units provided by the former Office of Inter-American Affairs for use in the other American republics have been used with outstanding success. Many of them have been worn out from constant operation over frequently difficult terrains and undeveloped roads. Experience with these units has been incorporated in a new mobile unit, 65 of which were purchased with fiscal year 1949 funds. The specially designed body is mounted on a "jeep" chassis which has been lengthened 10 inches. Built-in space is provided for all equipment and materials.

CARTOONS AS A WEAPON [6]

Hardhitting cartoons will play an increasingly important role in overall United States propaganda effort. As part of State Department's stepped-up "Truth Campaign," a million copies of a four-page, color cartoon leaflet on Korea, "The Korea Story," will soon be distributed in the Near and Middle East (may later go to Far East). Printed in four languages, it shows how Communists broke Potsdam pledge for a free Korea . . . were aggressors in South Korea.

To date, American cartoons have appeared in some 10,000 newspapers and magazines overseas. In some countries, newspapers display them on front pages . . . ; copies were cut out and posted on school and library bulletin boards . . . ; frequently readers enclose clippings in letters to friends behind Iron Curtain.

BALLETS AS PSYCHOLOGICAL WARFARE BULLETS [7]

Contracts have been signed at Paris for a three-month tour of South America by the American National Ballet Theatre. . . .

[6] From letter no325, *Public Relations News*, October 2, 1950. Reprinted with permission from *Public Relations News*, 815 Park Avenue, New York 21.

[7] From "American National Ballet Theatre to Tour South America." *Department of State Bulletin*. 24:700. April 30, 1951.

The company of 60 or more dancers and technicians will begin their tour on May 21 at Rio de Janeiro, officially opening the season at the Teatro Municipal Opera. After playing at Rio for three weeks, the Ballet Theatre will appear at São Paulo for another week. The option also calls for a four-week stay at Montevideo and Buenos Aires. The Department of State is co-operating with Ballet Theatre in arrangements for its tour as a means of demonstrating American cultural achievements to other countries.

CEYLON—NEWEST OUTPOST OF THE VOA [8]

The Voice of America has added a radio relay for broadcasts beamed to South Asia under an agreement just concluded between the government of South Ceylon and the government of United States, State Department announced this week. Under terms of the agreement, the United States will furnish and install "certain radio transmission and associated equipment for use by Radio Ceylon in return for certain facilities to be used by the government of Ceylon for the broadcast of VOA programs over Radio Ceylon," State said.

The Radio Ceylon facilities began relaying 30-minute Voice broadcasts Tuesday [May 15] in Hindi to India, and English to South Asia.

THE UNOFFICIAL "VOICES" OF AMERICA [9]

There is more than one American voice raised in international rebuttal of Soviet slander. Radio Free Europe [RFE], operated by the National Committee for a Free Europe, is a privately operated project with growing importance in the counter-propaganda warfare.

Recruiting many veterans of service in psychological warfare and the Office of Strategic Services, RFE began broadcasting

[8] From "Ceylon Transmitter," news story. *The Billboard*. 63:10. May 26, 1951. Reprinted by permission.

[9] From "Fighting Russian Radio Propaganda," by Gene Gleason, reporter, New York *Herald Tribune*. New York *Herald Tribune*. 111:14. June 22, 1951. Reprinted by permission.

Recruiting many veterans of service in psychological warfare and the Office of Strategic Services, RFE began broadcasting from a shortwave transmitter near Frankfurt in July 1950. Last month, it added a 135,000-watt medium-wave transmitter at Munich to beam its programs directly into Czechoslovakia.

General Lucius D. Clay, chairman of the Crusade for Freedom, . . . opened a national drive to raise three million dollars to expand the operations of Radio Free Europe. More . . . transmitters in Europe will be one phase of the expansion. . . .

Because it is a private agency, RFE [can] . . . shake off the . . . political and diplomatic restrictions on a government agency.

The World Wide Broadcasting Corporation, which leases a part of its international broadcasting time to the Voice of America, also has its own short-wave programs directed against the Soviet propaganda output.

Its five transmitters, located at Scituate, Mass., are the most powerful on the east coast, with one transmitter delivering 120,000 watts. Its best-known station is WRUL; the others are WRUS, WRUX, WRUW and WRUA. Walter S. Lemmon, president of World Wide and one of the pioneers in short-wave broadcasting, reports that his transmitters reach 56 countries.

During World War II, World Wide used its facilities to fight the Nazi broadcasts. In the years since then it has sent its crews into many American towns and cities, making broadcasts which presented the ordinary, every-day picture of American life to nations which had previously heard only the wild Soviet misrepresentations of our activities. World Wide also produced many educational programs for overseas listeners. It has stepped up its maximum power since the Soviet radio began the present propaganda campaign, and remains a potent force in the international short-wave field.

THE EDUCATIONAL EXCHANGE PROGRAM: DEVELOPMENT [10]

The educational exchange program of Public Law 402 was formally authorized on a worldwide scale in 1948. . . . Its basic

[10] From "Educational Exchange Among Free Nations," fifth semiannual report to Congress. United States Advisory Commission on Educational Exchange. *Department of State Bulletin.* 24:788-96. May 14, 1951.

concept was to interpret the United States to other countries. It was to make known the strength of the United States, the character and purpose of our people, and our national policies and objectives. At first restricted in the main to the Latin American countries as a continuation of what remained of the wartime program, the educational exchange service was expanded in 1950 to Europe and other areas of the Eastern Hemisphere. (The overseas library program has been worldwide ever since its beginning in World War II and it was a part of OWI as well as the Latin American program.)

The program was established with certain major instruments, including the exchange of persons, both at the student and mature leadership level, the maintenance of overseas libraries and cultural centers, the translation of representative American books and documents into foreign languages, assistance to American-sponsored schools in the other American republics, the support of various official projects in connection with universities, industrial exhibits, and fairs, and certain cooperative technological services in the Latin American area.

The concept of interpreting the United States appealed strongly to the American people, and the program has received wide public support and steadily increasing appropriations from the Congress. In 1948, a total of around $20 million was appropriated to the United States information and educational exchange programs, including the program of scientific and technical cooperation with the other American republics. Of this total of $20 million approximately $3 million was available for educational exchange activities.

In succeeding years the appropriations were made steadily larger. Funds available for 1951 exceed $111 million for the information and educational exchange programs of Public Law 402. Of this total around $10 million has been allocated to educational exchange. In addition, for fiscal year 1951, approximately $20 million in dollars and the dollar equivalent in foreign currencies is available for special educational exchange programs, such as the Fulbright educational program and other special programs in Finland and Germany, and the China area aid program.

THE EDUCATIONAL EXCHANGE PROGRAM: ADMINISTRATION [11]

The Secretary of State has the basic responsibility for the overall administration and management of the educational, cultural, scientific, and technical exchange program, hereinafter referred to as the educational and technical exchange program, which is carried out under the United States Information and Educational Exchange Act of 1948 (Public Law 402, 80th Congress). The programs and policies established by the Department of State for the execution of Public Law 402 are developed with the assistance of the United States Advisory Commission on Educational Exchange and its counterpart, the Advisory Commission on Information. . . .

The Secretary has been authorized to utilize the services, facilities, and personnel of other federal agencies in discharging his responsibilities under Public Law 402. Obviously the Department is not equipped for direct administration of the work in all fields of activity, and every attempt has been and will be made to secure the greatest amount of participation from other departments and agencies.

The Department of State provides guidance for the programs of the participating federal agencies in order that the government's multilateral and bilateral foreign-policy objectives may be carried out to the fullest extent by the execution of specific educational projects. This includes guidance and direction concerning global policy, the establishment of target areas, and the setting of general project priorities in the various areas of the world. . . .

In addition to its responsibility for overall administration of the program, the Department directly administers the educational and cultural operations—with one exception. The exchange of students and teachers is administered by the Federal Security Agency in cooperation with a private agency, the Institute of

[11] From *Trading Ideas with the World,* report of the United States Advisory Commission on Educational Exchange, March 31, 1949. Department of State Publication 3551. (International Information and Cultural Series 7). October 1949. p36-45.

International Education. All scientific and technical projects are administered directly by other agencies of the government.

Libraries

The objectives and purposes of the United States Libraries are to make immediately available under efficient conditions library and reference services to opinion-forming groups and to the general public of various countries. The libraries are so organized, staffed, and supplied as to present the best achievements of the American people and their intellectual production in culture and science.

The libraries are developed to serve best the specific needs and interests of the community in which each is located. . . .

The Department of State formulates policy for library service, coordinates such policy and programs, and maintains liaison with American public libraries, library associations, publishers, individual leaders, and members of the profession. It provides for the systematic supply of the United States Libraries with materials, books, pamphlets, magazines, newspapers, and other cultural and scientific materials and for analysis and evaluation of library operations. . . .

The libraries have proved to be valuable and essential in presenting the United States, its people, and its thinking to other peoples in an easily available and objective manner. In all countries where they are maintained the libraries have served to provide information regarding the United States and to counteract propaganda adverse to the interests of this country; in many countries they have provided the main channel of approach to influential groups and individuals with whom it is most desirable to maintain contact.

Cultural Centers

The Department of State assisted in maintaining 30 cultural centers established in the other American republics. These institutions originated as the result of cooperation among nationals of host countries and Americans resident there, and, in some cases, with the participation of the Department. These centers offer library facilities, lectures, concerts, exhibits, and motion pictures, teach English and the language of the country, and sponsor social activities which bring Americans and nationals into direct contact. The Institute's Branch provides program guidance, American teaching and administrative personnel, books and cultural materials, and grants to defray deficits when the centers' local income does not cover operating expenses. Binational cultural societies outside the Western Hemisphere are occasionally given assistance in the form of materials, guidance, and encouragement, but this program has operated essentially in Latin America only.

The chief activity of the centers has been the teaching of English to nationals and Spanish and Portuguese to United States citizens. Fees for language instruction cover the major portion of the local operating costs. Other local income is derived from dues paid by members. In some cases contributions from local American business firms and host governments increase the centers' financial self-sufficiency.

In view of the annual nature of appropriations, the Department has thus far encouraged the centers to develop revenue-producing activities to the end that the essential portion of their work might go on even if appropriations should be seriously curtailed. In 1942, when the Department originally undertook the guidance of this program, the centers were producing approximately 10 per cent of the total cost of their operation. In the calendar year 1947 the total income of the centers, $639,627, accounted for 95 per cent of local operating costs and 61 per cent of total operating costs.

The Department of State covers 5 per cent local operating deficit through grants-in-aid and provides American administrators to help with the smooth performance of the operations. The centers are also provided with qualified American teachers who furnish instruction in English and information on American life. The Department services the centers with books for their libraries and provides teaching aids and other materials.

Aid to Schools

During 1948 assistance was provided to private, nonprofit, American-sponsored community schools in the American republics to help insure that such institutions would reflect the best in American educational methods, goals, and equipment. This assistance was extended to these schools by the American Council on Education under contract with the Department of State in the form of (1) grants of money usually for use by the schools in paying salaries of American teachers, (2) educational materials, and (3) professional services, including a teacher-placement service.

Approximately 270 such educational institutions, patterned after the primary and secondary schools in the United States, provided American residents and foreign nations of Latin America with American-type education. . . .

Book Exhibits

A number of traveling book exhibits were developed during 1947 and 1948. Whenever possible the itineraries for these traveling exhibits are planned to coincide with the timing of annual international book fairs and conferences in various cities. For the most part the cultural centers and American libraries serve as focal points for showing the exhibits. The exhibits are shown in provincial cities as well as in capitals, through cooperation with ministries of education and other interested organizations. Eventually, the books included in the traveling exhibits either come to rest in the cultural centers and United States libraries or are presented to appropriate local institutions, thus becoming permanently available to the reading public.

Traveling exhibits are designed to demonstrate a subject field or a segment of United States scientific, scholarly, or literary production. Representative exhibits are (1) a collection of Americana, chosen for its pictorial excellence, including outstanding examples of fine bookmaking, children's literature, books on contemporary architecture, housing, city planning, arts and crafts, and books on the American scene; (2) a collection of representative textbooks for elementary and secondary schools and of educational books on theory, principles, methods, and philosophy of education; (3) a collection of books issued by university presses; (4) a collection of recent children's books, chosen for their literary and pictorial excellence and for their portrayal of life in the United States; (5) a graphic-arts collection, chosen from the annual selections of the American Institute of Graphic Arts to represent fine bookmaking; and (6) a collection of recent books in many subject fields, with emphasis on scientific, medical, and technical titles, which was first displayed at the United Nations Educational, Scientific and Cultural Organization conference in Mexico City in November 1947. . . .

Translations

The translation program covers the whole field of cooperation. It provides—in the languages of the countries where they are to be used—textbooks and handbooks for use in connection with scientific and technical projects; general informational material to aid and supplement cooperative undertakings related to education, agriculture, public health, and social welfare; and books on history, literature, and art to assist the peoples of various countries in becoming acquainted with and understanding one another. Both government and nongovernment publications are translated and printed. . . .

Exchange Programs

The exchange of professors, leaders, and specialists . . . is directly administered by the Department of State. The program for exchange of students and teachers, as distinguished from professors and specialists, is conducted by the Department of State in cooperation with the Office of Education of the Federal Security Agency and the Institute of International Education, a private agency. Under this program there are two types of student exchange, both involving the expenditure of United States Government funds: (1) those provided under the convention for the promotion of inter-American cultural relations, signed at Buenos Aires in 1936, which authorizes a reciprocal exchange of two graduate students every year between the signatory governments, and (2) the exchange of graduate students between the United States and each of the other American republics under Public Law 402. In connection with both types of exchange, provision is made for placement, counsel, guidance and orientation. These services are rendered by grants-in-aid to private agencies, under contract to the Department of State.

Students selected under this program are chosen on the basis of individual merit, potential value to the United States, the educational, cultural, and economic needs of their countries, relative values of chosen fields of study, and a knowledge of the language of the country. Grants are awarded with no distinction as to race, creed, or color. In the selection of American students, preference is given to veterans of the armed services. . . .

Under the provisions of Public Law 584 of the 79th Congress (the Fulbright Act), local currency in various foreign countries made available to the United States under surplus-property sales agreements may be utilized for educational exchange purposes. An executive agreement is negotiated with each foreign government to establish the financial arrangements and to provide for the creation of a United States Educational Foundation. The boards of directors of these foundations include United States citizens as well as foreign nationals.

PRIVATE ENTERPRISE WEAPONS [12]

Your government recognizes that, in order to achieve the objectives of its foreign policy throughout the world, it must have the cooperation of private enterprise and private organizations whose daily relationships with people in foreign lands contribute to the building of international good will. . . .

Our information and cultural program is under the direction of the Assistant Secretary for Public Affairs, Edward Barrett. It is administered by Charles Hulten, the General Manager, who conducts operations through the Office of International Information and the Office of Educational Exchange. We have more than 600 Public Affairs officers attached to our 142 diplo-

[12] From "The American Idea: Package It for Export," by John M. Begg, Director, Private Enterprise Corporation, International Information and Educational Exchange Program. *Department of State Bulletin.* 24:409-12. March 12, 1951.

matic and consular missions throughout the world. It is through them that we conduct regional and local operations. They are our direct contact with the people overseas. It is through this framework that the Private Enterprise Staff aids and cooperates with business organizations and civic groups in helping to carry the Campaign of Truth to the people of the world.

Companies doing business overseas have been able to help us—and, in many cases, we have been able to help them. Companies selling products overseas can also sell America and our concept of freedom. A great many are doing it today. For one thing, they know that improved living standards create a demand for more and better goods; and, in most cases, these business organizations in foreign lands are key factors in community life. It is through their representatives that America is largely judged, public opinion molded, and international good will obtained.

Some American companies which advertise in foreign publications have adapted their copy to help sell the American idea abroad. . . . This idea of selling America through advertising copy lends itself to commercially sponsored broadcasts abroad, to posters and window cards, to pamphlets and leaflets. The field is so broad that there is really no end to the media through which business and industry can help sell the truth abroad. . . . The Department of State cooperated with the Advertising Council in publishing a booklet entitled *Advertising, A New Weapon in the World Fight for Freedom.* It is a guide for American business firms advertising overseas. . . .

A number of companies are including leaflets, printed cards, and other informative material in the thousands of letters which they send abroad in the course of a year. One manufacturer is including picture cards of historic America in his product in South America. . . . One large company . . . in Chicago, and many more throughout the country, have urged their employees to send their company magazines to friends and relatives overseas. Others have sponsored the collection of used magazines for shipment to our information centers overseas where they are distributed.

From every walk of life and from all parts of America, men, women, and children are writing letters overseas. These messages from Main Street, from the hearts of Americans, are telling our story in the surest way that it can be told. This great project is sponsored by the Common Council for American Unity. It has rallied the foreign language press and radio in this country in support of the most dramatic personal appeal for peace any people have ever undertaken. . . . Last year, nearly a million dollars' worth of books were sent overseas through the CARE organization. . . . Many years ago, the pioneer companies in foreign trade discovered that it pays dividends to bring foreign employees to this country for training and education. Today, numerous companies offer scholarships to worthy students in American universities and conduct continuous exchange programs for their workers. . . .

CURRENT STRATEGY IN THE WAR OF IDEAS

EDITOR'S INTRODUCTION

The keynote of American propaganda is "the truth." While the Campaign of Truth called for by President Truman in February 1950 officially opened the psychological warfare offensive against international communism, the "strategy of truth" has been a guiding principle in all previous propaganda efforts by the United States, at least officially. This cannot be said to have been solely for ethical reasons. The phrase "the truth will out" or "truth will prevail" are common doctrines throughout modern democratic experience. "Truth" was the basis of the directives of the OWI both at home and abroad, and of military propaganda used against Germany and Japan in the field.

This has had some unfortunate results, due chiefly to interpretation. Propaganda theory emphasizes the importance of truth strategy, but likewise emphasizes the value of selectivity. Telling the whole truth, presenting both the favorable and the unfavorable points, may and often does weaken the effectiveness of the propaganda story. And considerable controversy has centered over this one issue. Propagandists whose previous training was in the field of news reporting tend to take the literal view of presenting "all the news." Those whose training has been in the social sciences or such persuasive "sciences" as advertising have readily espoused the cause of editorial selection or "slanting" the news for the desired effect. It should be noted here that at least until after the inauguration of the Campaign of Truth early in 1950 the emphasis was upon news and information only. The theory apparently was that presenting the facts was sufficient.

But psychological warfare implies, even requires, the use of psychological techniques. The aim is to *persuade*. This in turn implies a much more complicated operation than a mere international "news bureau." Before the process of persuading can take place, the propagandist has to learn all he can about his audience—to know what they already believe and what they *will* believe. This was given the resounding label of "comparative national psychology" by the Nazis, who made much of it in developing their propaganda theory but fortunately failed to apply it very effectively in World War II.

Then, with knowledge of the audience at hand, the propagandist has the job of fitting the facts at his disposal into the most effective propaganda style. Part of this job is selecting the particular facts that will have the greatest appeal to the audience, yet most effectively tell the story the propagandist desires to convey. In some countries, simple newscasts via the Voice of America may be sufficient. In others, rumor or jokes ridiculing the particular group in power may be far more effective.

Developing a strategy for psychological warfare is not an easy task. It is even more difficult in a democracy where the propagandist is operating in the open, subject to constant review and criticism by the representatives of the public: both Congress and the press of the nation. As more and more attention has been focused upon the psychological warfare campaign of the United States, everyone has felt free to criticize the propaganda themes and their effectiveness. Yet with the exception of a small handful of persons outside the Department of State, the actual strategy in current use is highly secret. In fact, the chief reason Secretary of State Acheson gave for wishing to withhold publication of the Formosa policy directive (see Appendix for text) which figured so prominently in the MacArthur Senate investigation recently, was that publication would provide the Russians with further propaganda ammunition that the United States was "slanting" news in its "Campaign of Truth." While anyone familiar with propaganda would realize that "slanting" news in a desired direction is customary, publication of a directive indicating how it was to be done in a specific situation, according to Acheson, would be proof that the United States was "slanting" its news. This one directive is the only one known to have been released publicly.

Strategy involves two things: development of basic themes to govern propaganda and the utilization of various techniques to make that propaganda effective. While not too much is available as to how current strategy is formulated, it seems logical to assume that the procedure would be very much like that of the Office of War Information.

In handling information during the war, the OWI relied upon *plans* and *directives*, according to Charles A. H. Thomson's account in *Overseas Information Service of the United States Government.* Plans were designed to "set forth the background of propaganda and information operations to a given area, to describe the media available for such operations, to estimate the characteristics of the propaganda targets, to set forth propaganda objectives, aims, and themes," and were long-range in nature. Weekly directives supplemented these general plans on a short-term basis. In addition, daily instruction sheets controlled each day's operations in line with the weekly directives. Special instructions were issued whenever a situation arose which could not be covered in any of the regular procedures.

While by no means complete, this chapter sums up strategy pronouncements released officially by the Department of State and offers a number of examples of techniques currently in use in the war of ideas.

ORIGINS OF INFORMATION STRATEGY: 1945 MACMAHON REPORT[1]

The adequacy with which the United States as a society is portrayed to the other peoples of the world is a matter of concern to the American people and their government. . . . Modern international relations lie between peoples, not merely governments. Statements on foreign policy are intelligible abroad in the spirit in which they are intended only when other peoples understand the context of national tradition and character which is essential to the meaning of any statement. This is especially true of a collaborative foreign policy which by nature must be open and popular, understood and accepted at home and abroad.

International information activities are integral to the conduct of foreign policy. The object of such activities is, first, to see that the context of knowledge among other peoples about the United States is full and fair, not meager and distorted, and, second, to see that the policies which directly affect other peoples are presented abroad with enough detail as well as background to make them understandable.

THE STRATEGY OF TRUTH[2]

As people with a personal stake in international affairs, and as Americans, you and I are up against a rough assignment—perhaps the roughest in the history of this nation. While we are trying to build a peace, and while we are pushing toward this objective, we have to fight a cold war with a ruthless and unprincipled adversary. . . .

The scene of this conflict is a sick and confused world. Part of this world is struggling to recover from the ravages of the Second World War in 40 years. Other areas carry on a ceaseless

[1] By Arthur W. Macmahon, consultant on administration to the State Department. *Memorandum on the Postwar International Information Program of the United States.* Department of State Publication 2438. 1945. p xi-xii.

[2] From "Expanding Techniques for a Truth Strategy," by Edward W. Barrett, Assistant Secretary for Public Affairs, United States Department of State. *Department of State Bulletin.* 23:945-8. December 11, 1950.

battle against worn-out land, disease, and ignorance—merely to exist. Many peoples who have been quiescent, apathetic, or impotent under alien rule are now responding to an urge for nationalist expression of some sort. There are varying degrees of popular discontent and, in many places, a vague demand for change—any change, just so long as it is different. . . . One characteristic of the situation . . . operates to the temporary advantage of the Soviet Union. Confusion and instability are made to order for their various techniques. . . .

The United States is compelled to follow a far slower procedure. We have discovered that progressive ideas concerning freedom . . . can't be imposed upon others. We know that freedom can develop only out of local conviction and experience. We can only spell out the meaning of freedom and, by persuasion, dissemination of information, and example, demonstrate its worth. Thus, we are politically less mobile than our adversary —a handicap of the moment which, in the long run, will be offset by the durability of the product we are exporting. . . .

Soviet propaganda is a major weapon in the Kremlin's political arsenal. Here again, their disregard for truth gives them great latitude of operation. They can slant their output in any direction, regardless of the facts. They can distort and twist to their hearts' content. . . .

However, a close and penetrating inspection of both the Kremlin's system and its weapons and tactics in the cold war reveals grave weaknesses. What the Soviets still present to the world as a revolutionary society is actually one of extreme reaction. The counterrevolution took place hard on the heels of the revolt that overthrew the czars, and, instead of being led from serfdom to freedom, the Russian people went from serfdom to slavery. This contradiction is a point of vulnerability which can be exploited with damaging effect.

The Kremlin rulers, themselves, are very much aware of this weak point. They are afraid to permit large numbers of their people to compare their own conditions with those in the free world. The troops that moved into Western Europe at the end of World War II had to be brought back to the Soviet Union for a lengthy reindoctrination—and, in many instances, the stronger medicine of the purge. This fear of comparison is the reason for the Iron Curtain. The political or social organism that requires total isolation from its neighbors cannot be regarded as a strong organism. It is simply too vulnerable to the truth.

A second major weakness of the Soviet Union lies in the basic deception in the Soviet world campaign. The Soviet is peddling its revolution to peoples motivated by a desire for liberty and a greater voice in the handling of their own affairs. By craft and subterfuge, Soviet propaganda presents communism and its revolutionary techniques as a package deal for realizing that desire. In those areas where people have been taken in by the Soviet sales campaign, disillusionment sets in early. The people soon discover they have been gulled by a group of pitiless twentieth century imperialists. That is why we today have a team at work gathering and reporting to the Voice all possible facts as to what really went on in the Communist colony of North Korea.

From start to finish, the Kremlin strategy is wide open to effective counterattack. The ingrained dishonesty of the Soviet promises as compared to their intentions can be unmasked and spotlighted. The soft spot here is identical with that in the Soviet organization itself. It cannot stand against the truth.

Now, what of our own capabilities? To begin with, we are strong where the Soviets are weak. The independence and the freedom which we have preserved for ourselves and which we are trying to extend is the hallmark of a solid and a strong organization. Moreover, we have the great advantage of not wanting anything from anyone. We seek neither power nor domain. We have declared our purposes. We want lasting peace, an improvement in the world standard of living to be brought about by international collaboration. We are, finally, basically committed to individual rights and human freedom. When we talk in such terms, we speak a universal language which has at least some meaning for all men.

Consequently, it is obvious that the most telling weapon we can bring to bear on the Soviet Union in this war of ideas is an information program—or propaganda program if you want to call it that—which deals exclusively in facts. And I mean all the facts. We've got to expand and develop this Campaign of Truth. This is the weapon which has the firepower to pierce the Iron Curtain. This is the weapon that has the explosive force to rip the camouflage from the Soviet position and reveal it as it truly is —a stronghold of reaction and imperialism.

OBJECTIVES OF AMERICAN STRATEGY [3]

There are those, today, who say we should plaster the countryside of Europe with American billboards and send American sound trucks blaring through continental villages. Anyone who really knows Europe today knows that this would do more harm than good. It would simply support the present tendency of too many Europeans to think that the current conflict is basically just one of the United States versus the USSR. And it would permit the enemies of freedom to shout that we are "just trying to buy the minds of men with American dollars."

Instead of this flamboyant approach, we feel much greater progress can be made in other ways: first, by telling our story forthrightly over the Voice of America and our other media; second, by sponsoring large-scale visits to this country by leaders of thought in other nations; third, by encouraging and assisting like-minded groups in other countries to mount large-scale, home-grown campaigns to expose Kremlin communism and drive home the reasons for strength and unity in the free world.

A very large part of our work today consists of stimulating and encouraging and assisting organizations and groups abroad to join in the Campaign of Truth. There is nothing tricky about this. All the organizations concerned are groups who see the world picture as we see it. But they do need stimulation, help, ideas and assistance of many kinds. We are ready, willing, and able to provide such cooperation. There are, today, hundreds of pieces of literature that have resulted from just such joint cooperative activities.

[3] From "Counteract Defeatism by Winning the Cold War," by Edward W. Barrett, Assistant Secretary for Public Affairs, United States Department of State. *Department of State Bulletin*. 24:408. March 12, 1951.

At the risk of oversimplifying, we can say that we have four chief objectives: (1) Exposing to the world, directly and indirectly, the truly reactionary, vicious and phony nature of Kremlin communism; (2) building up a spirit of unity, spunk, determination and confidence in all the nations of the free world; (3) inculcating in other peoples a readiness and desire to cooperate with America—by disproving Soviet lies about us and by making clear that we are a resolute, strong, and honest nation whose moral strength and physical strength can be counted on; (4) building, behind the Iron Curtain, psychological obstacles to further Kremlin aggression.

Are we hitting the target? I think the actions of the Soviets themselves are one of the best proofs of this. They employ a thousand-odd transmitters in a gigantic effort to block us; they splatter their papers and fill their radios with violent attacks on what we say.

"TARGETING"—KEY PRINCIPLE [4]

One of the most important factors in the intensified Campaign of Truth is the increased attention given to "targeting." . . . Targets vary from country to country but all output, whether it be the printed word, motion pictures, radio or exchange of persons, is tailored for specific key target groups.

In Southeast Asia, our answer to the Big Lie is targeted primarily at the great masses. In Indochina, for example, a major campagn is under way to tell the Vietnamese the true story of Communist Ho Chi-minh, who has represented himself as a friendly land reformer. Here, the problem is one of awakening the deluded masses to the evils of Communist infiltration. In reaching these masses where illiteracy is high, the program makes wide use of simple visual techniques—cartoons, posters, and motion pictures.

In this business of pin-pointing our objectives, of targeting the program, the two-way exchange of people is one of the best

[4] From "Our Answer to the Big Lie," by William C. Johnstone, Jr., Director, Office of Educational Exchange. *Department of State Bulletin.* 24:370-4. March 5, 1951.

weapons in our arsenal of truth. It is an accurate weapon in destroying the Big Lie. It can hit the target with tremendous power.

When the Communists tell the people of France or Italy or Belgium, for instance, that labor is not free in the United States —that the workers are only tools of the greedy capitalist, we can invite a labor leader to come to the United States and see for himself. We've done that many times. . . .

Exchanges . . . are effectively countering Communist lies and creating pro-American attitudes. For example, a Far Eastern journalist, whose paper had often carried virulent anti-American articles, returned to write a series of favorable stories about America . . . [and] this paper was using 50 per cent more of the output of the Campaign of Truth than heretofore.

GUIDES TO VOA STRATEGY [5]

In a democracy . . . the word and the deed must go together. Pure propaganda at variance with acts may serve to confuse for a while or even to attain immediate tactical objectives. But in the long run false pretensions will out. In fact, it is one of our constant purposes to expose the false pretensions of our opponents. By the same token it is our basic rule to maintain credibility and confidence in the Voice of America, even at the expense of occasional tactical reverses.

In our programs to the peoples of the captive states . . . we try to give them the assurance that we have not forgotten and will not forget. We try to sustain their hope for eventual freedom and encourage their continued hostility toward and their resistance to their oppressors. At the same time we must avoid arousing their hopes unduly and thus disillusion them. We must also avoid inviting them to commit suicide by premature rebellion. It is a fine line to draw. We are constantly attacked by extremist emigré groups for being either too soft or too hard. Maybe this in itself is a good indication that we are continuing to maintain the right line, but a lot of other more valid evidence indicates this too. . . .

[5] From "Effectiveness of the Voice of America," address by Foy D. Kohler, Chief, International Broadcasting Division, before the Institute for Education by Radio-Television, Columbus, Ohio, May 4, 1951.

In our programs to the Soviet Union, we draw a clear distinction and do our best to drive a wedge between the despotic regime and its enslaved subjects. We appeal to their memories of better days and remind them of their own suppressed historic traditions and political and literary classics. We stimulate their skepticism about the story being told them by their own rulers, by telling them the other half. We try to clarify the curiosity we know they have about the outer world, and correct the warped and distorted image of that world given them by their Kremlin masters.

BROADCAST APPROACH FOR IRON CURTAIN COUNTRIES [6]

The Voice's output . . . directed behind the Iron Curtain is made up of about half hard-hitting, well-selected news and about half commentary—material clearly reflecting the American point of view and labeled as such. Logic, irony, and plain cold economic facts each play their role in the commentaries. For example, the potential might of the free world as opposed to the potential strength of the Communist world is an important argument today. Humor, too, also plays a part from time to time. For example, we had a lot of fun and did an effective job, I believe, with the Communist allegation that we were dropping potato bugs behind the Iron Curtain. We had even more fun and effect, I believe, in later reporting the Czechoslovak wisecrack that the Americans were now finding it necessary to drop potatoes in order to keep the potato bugs alive.

MEANS OF DETERMINING STRATEGY [7]

The best way to improve our output is to study and follow closely the reactions of the actual target audience. Today, we still seek and value the advice of experts—or even so-called experts—

[6] From "Stressing Information Themes to Meet Changing World Conditions," by Edward W. Barrett, Assistant Secretary for Public Affairs, United States Department of State. *Department of State Bulletin.* 24:13-15. January 1, 1951.

[7] From "Stressing Information Themes to Meet Changing World Conditions," by Edward W. Barrett, Assistant Secetary for Public Affairs, United States Department of State. *Department of State Bulletin.* 24:13-15. January 1, 1951.

in this country, but we are placing far more value on the opinions and reactions of the audience concerned. We survey, by tested sampling methods, the reactions of the audiences in nations that are open to us. We organize panels representing a cross section of the population; we have them sample our output and answer questions from us. In the more inaccessible zones, we get regular reaction reports from our embassy staffs and from others who are in a position to advise us. We systematically interrogate escapees from these areas and organize them into panels from time to time. I repeat—we feel that such steps as these are the real proof of the pudding and the real guide to continuing improvement in our output.

RIAS—THE TRUTH CRUSADER [8]

Last spring . . . Soviet Zone officials, backed by the Communist-dominated press and radio, launched a campaign of bitter invective, rolling up their heavy propaganda guns to train them against RIAS, the Radio in the American Sector [operated by the Office of the United States High Commissioner for Germany], the station which because of its unique position—105 miles within the Soviet Zone border—has become the only powerful voice of truth behind the Iron Curtain. . . .

But RIAS listening is a dangerous pastime in the East German police state. For this reason the nightly RIAS show produced especially for the Soviet Zone, "Berlin Speaks to the Zone," has been toned down in production and moderated to a placid pitch. The *pièce de résistance* of RIAS' twenty and one half hours daily program fare, this broadcast was formerly aired with all the approved hoopla and fanfare that good sound effects can contrive. Today, at the request of Eastern listeners themselves, the show has been toned down so that no loud or symbolic acoustic effects identify it to nosy neighbors.

Three times daily, six days a week, this 15-minute spot acquaints clandestine listeners with daily events in East Germany

[8] From article by Aileen S. Miles, staff writer. *Information Bulletin*, the Office of the United States High Commissioner for Germany. December 1950. p3-6.

which Communist censorship has withheld and brings them vital information necessary in their struggle against totalitarianism. An anathema to Communist leaders, the program's famous "spy lists" bring froth to the lips of the party's faithful. Soviet agents—butcher, baker or well-known university professor—known as Communist spies are named by the American station and listeners are warned to avoid the spy in their midst lest he denounce them to the authorities for disciplinary action or a one-way ticket to the uranium mines in Eastern Germany.

Neatly drawn word-portraits of public figures in Soviet Zone activities show East listeners the quality of the men being placed in high positions over the "People's Democracy." When Vincenz Mueller, former German general, was named as leader of the NDP (East zone political party serving as a catch-all for former Nazis), RIAS dug into the records and found a particularly unpleasant one attached to the general substantiating his reputation for ruthless and unscrupulous acts.

And, again, when Karl-Fritz Bernhardt, leader of the "Society for Soviet-German Friendship," was nominated to lead a discussion on the evils of RIAS, it was found that Bernhardt was a singularly unfortunate choice. On the following evening's show to the Soviet Zone, RIAS featured a certified copy of Bernhardt's court record, the first chapter of which was written in 1922, containing his spaced-out convictions through the years for theft, libel, fraud, perjury and other offenses.

Reaction to the program has gratified the RIAS staff. Letters and telephone calls pour into the station begging for repeats on special shows and showering praise on the fillip RIAS is providing to resistance workers in the East. . . .

[When] RIAS warned Soviet Zone listeners on June 29, 1950, that mills and grain storerooms would be subject to strict inspection the following morning, one listener wrote: "The announcement saved not only my father, but a number of others in the same business from having their mills closed or perhaps expropriated. What RIAS means to us business people in the Soviet Zone is something we only can judge."

Providing the satirical twist to humor so beloved by German audiences, the show for the Soviet Zone takes a lighter twist each

Saturday when Comrade Otto Pieckewitz—the "200 per cent Communist" clown—goes on the air to argue Communist ideology to its illogical conclusions. RIAS dreamed up this now famous character to help East Germans laugh and he has proved so successful that when he was taken off the air last September, a stream of letters from the Soviet Zone insisted on the return of Pieckewitz, who is now a regular weekly feature.

When the Communists accused the United States of dropping potato bugs from airplanes to destroy the East German potato crop, Pieckewitz was appointed "Special People's Controller for the Liquidation of the Imperialistic Potato Bug." To the delight of East listeners, the stodgy Pieckewitz spumed over the seditious joke being circulated in the Russian zone that the American Society for the Prevention of Cruelty to Animals was petitioning to have potatoes dropped on the East zone so that the bugs would have something to eat.

No Communist slogan is too obtuse for Pieckewitz to explain as he burlesques the Communist credo. His explanation of the Soviet Zone import-export program is worthy of a Russian economist: "We sell bricks to Italy in exchange for lemons. The lemons go to Denmark for butter. We trade the butter to Sweden for steel. We send the steel to Russia in exchange for clay which we use to manufacture more bricks for Italy. . . ." The pompous Pieckewitz, gulping "socialized aspirin tablets" at every setback to the Communist cause, has won the hearts of his listeners. As the typical Communist petty official, the self-important, sluggish-witted Pieckewitz is a natural for ridicule—and no matter how heavily it is spread the German audience loves it.

But it is the straight news broadcasts that American authorities credit as the most powerful programs for building up the vast listening audience which RIAS boasts today. [After] . . . years of the Hitler-imposed news blackout and the ensuing Soviet clamp down, the people of Eastern Germany for the first time in 17 years are today learning the facts behind what their neighbors are doing and thinking.

Tying closely with President Truman's truth campaign to the uninformed peoples of the Iron Curtain countries, RIAS is taking the place of a local free press and is carrying objective world and domestic news into the homes of the news-hungry people of Eastern Germany. Especially designed Soviet Zone programs feature stories deliberately omitted from the Eastern press—news on Western developments in the world picture, glimpses into the free press and editorial comment from Atlantic Pact nations.

Putting over its important product, RIAS is following accepted radio techniques in casting the bait of excellent entertainment, good dance bands, dramatic shows and sports to snare its prospective customers into the RIAS listening habit. Berlin bobbysoxers—once grist for the Hitler Youth mill—are now getting joy through bebop as they tune into RIAS jam sessions while West Berlin schools are hooked into a RIAS radio school of the air which departs from many formalized educational methods.

Americanizations have gone over with Berlin listeners to such a degree that among the most popular daytime programs is a strictly U.S.-style soap opera depicting the fortunes and adversities of a typical Berlin family and their daily coping with existence in the four-sector city.

As an instrument for internationalism, the station is acquainting German audiences with cultural life in the United States as well as political thought through two Voice of America broadcasts relayed daily, while a bi-weekly ECA show points up the varied cultures of Germany's neighbors who are participating in the European Recovery Program.

In its zeal for entertainment, RIAS maintains strong emphasis on broadcasting public service features. Youth programs stress understanding of civic institutions; Berlin's city council is given regular air time in an effort to promote Berliners' interest in their government, while the city's welfare funds are swelled by the proceeds from special shows staged by RIAS for this purpose. For RIAS not only serves as a symbol of hope for the Eastern zone but also as the community station for western Berliners and in this role must prepare its programs for public service.

Among the innovations used by the station to increase its effectiveness during the past year was the development of a telephone news service providing a three-minute newscast to anyone in Greater Berlin dialing No. 23. During July, telephone officials reported that since the outbreak of the Korean conflict the number of calls placed daily for the RIAS telephone newscast had jumped from 12,000 to 18,000—more than half of them originating from the Soviet Sector of Berlin.

Gradually and almost imperceptibly over the years, RIAS has weaned its listeners from the Communist-controlled Radio Berlin until today's latest surveys show that 98 per cent of the West Berlin radio audience is listening to the American station. . . .

RIAS came into being in the early part of the experiment in four-power occupation of Germany. . . . When West Berliners planned a protest meeting [against the Berlin blockade] on September 9, 1948, and wanted sympathizers to gather before the ruins of the old Reichstag building to voice their condemnation of the Soviet blockade and the attempt to implant a totalitarian regime, RIAS spread the news of the meeting throughout the city. Within a few hours of the idea, the city was rallying to the call broadcast by the station and 250,000 persons, workers, men and women—outraged and angry—dropped their work and rushed to the meeting determined to make their voices heard.

With the end of the blockade American authorities felt it was now time to give a stellar role to RIAS in the all-important East-West drama being staged in the politically sliced-up city. A powerful, modern 100,000-watt German transmitter was purchased for RIAS, placing the station on a par with all the powerful European medium-wave transmitters and vastly improving the reception of Eastern Germany with its 18 million population. Because of frequency difficulties, RIAS' range was restricted until March 15, 1950, when, operating on a new and favorable frequency, it became audible throughout Europe at night.

Swinging into its stronger political stride, the station stepped up its programming to a sustained intensive pitch. . . . A daily editorial meeting attended by both American and German staffers establishes the political work-load for the day. Domestic politics and economic trends are carefully sifted, special events broadcasts outlined, and commentaries and other political features shaped up. Representatives from the program department coordinate their output with those from the political department. Weekly, the same staff members get together to discuss the broader political and long-range program planning. . . .

This, then, is RIAS: The radio station which is known as a symbol of truth to those who live behind the veil of censorship.

SENATOR MUNDT ON VOICE STRATEGY [9]

Question: Just what are we trying to do with the Voice of America? Are we primarily trying to stir the Russian people to revolt?

Senator Mundt: No, I think not. . . . Insofar as we've broadcast behind the Iron Curtain, especially into Russia, we do it with the intent in mind of making the Russian people realize that our quarrel is with their leaders, and not with the people of Russia. . . .

Question: What do we expect those Russian listeners to do about that situation though?

Mundt: We expect them to do a great many things which they can do. One of them very definitely is not to revolt at this time, but we do expect them to sort of soldier on the job, to slow down in the defense activities, to fail to respond to 5-year programs which would step up production on the farm and in the factories. We expect them, on occasion, as they have, to pull out of Russia and to escape to a free country and to come here so that we can learn from Russians who know what kind of defense establishments they're building behind the Urals and in the defense centers of Russia.

Question: You say, Senator, that we're not asking them to revolt. But are we coming right out and asking them in plain and simple language to—well, that is, loaf on the job—to slow down?

[9] From "Reporters' Roundup: How Good Is the Voice of America?" radio broadcast by Senator Karl E. Mundt and others over the Mutual Broadcasting System, March 15, 1951. *Congressional Record*. 97:A1763-5. March 30, 1951.

Mundt: No, I think that our job is primarily . . . to drive a wedge of suspicion between the ordinary Russian . . . and the government gauleiter who goes around as one of the Communist high command, and if we can constantly keep in the minds of—say—a hundred and ninety of the hundred and ninety-five million Russians, a big suspicion that their politicians over there are not doing right by them—they'll think of their own ways of trying to get even with the Kremlin and the Communist command.

Question: How are we going to impart that suspicion, though? Isn't it reasonable to believe that the Russians will have the same attitude toward our propaganda broadcast that we would have—say—in this country toward Russian propaganda?

Mundt: Not if we continue our present policy, which is to keep the broadcasts factual. What we try to do is to tell the truth about America in the conviction that the truth about America is better than any fiction that a Communist storybook writer could write about Russia, and if we establish credibility in the minds of the Russians, I think we have achieved a great deal. . . .

Question: Isn't it true that we are largely on the defensive on the Voice of America? . . .

Mundt: I think there is a lot of validity to that criticism. . . . Certainly, I would like to have them become much more positive and get off the defensive. . . . We should get over on the positive to the greatest extent possible. On the other hand, we must never stop answering the slanderous falsehoods that the propagandists of Moscow continuously drill into the unsuspecting ears of the people of Europe. . . .

Question: But just how do you take the offensive? What do you tell them?

Mundt: You tell them the truth about America. You tell them what it means to have trial by jury. You tell them what it means to have freedom of religion and freedom of speech. You tell them what it means when you go to a polling place to have a choice between two or three or four candidates. You tell them what private ownership means, and the thrill that you get from farming your own piece of soil instead of the state's piece of soil. That's what I mean about getting on the affirmative.

Question: That seems to me like that's still defensive. . . .

Mundt: Well, that's what I would say . . . would be a program of offense. . . . I think that you do that, however, more successfully if there's some subtlety in connection with it. I think if it becomes too obviously propaganda that you're not nearly as successful as if you plant these seeds of doubt and suspicion in the hearts of the people behind the Iron Curtain as against their government, giving them a sort of a feeling of homesickness for the days when they did have a chance to go to church, when they did have a chance for private ownership, when they did have a chance for freedom of speech. I think those in the long run are more effective than simply to engage in a cantankerous argument against the philosophical and theoretical practice of communism.

BROADCASTS ON KOREA [10]

Following is a summary of VOA play on the Korea story from the 25th of June through the 1st of July [1950] . . . the first week of the Korean war. The . . . figure given represents the . . . percentage of total time allotted to news and commentary by VOA [which was devoted to the Korean war]:

Date	Percentage
June 25:	52.3 per cent
June 26:	72.9 per cent
June 27:	81 per cent
June 28:	83.1 per cent
June 29:	73.9 per cent
June 30:	82.2 per cent
July 1:	79.2 per cent

. . . Certain language units, like the Polish, for instance, were broadcasting at that same time in addition to the Korean war news items related to it. Thus the Polish desk had on June 25, 20 per cent of its output devoted to the Soviet policy of aggression; on June 26, 17 per cent to the same topic; on June 30,

[10] From a report on broadcasts concerning the Korean incident read during debate on VOA appropriations measure by Representative John J. Rooney of New York. *Congressional Record.* 96:13731-2. August 26, 1950.

11 per cent of its total output devoted to Soviet policy of aggression.

On June 27, on the occasion of the presidential announcement regarding United States action in Korea, a special transmission to the Far East was instituted immediately upon receipt of the presidential announcement shortly after 12 noon, and broadcasting continued in English, Korean, Mandarin, and Cantonese from shortly after 12 noon through the entire afternoon and evening. For your further information, the central news section was servicing the language desk during the week from June 25 through July 1 as follows:

June 25: 619 lines out of an approximate total of 1,500.
June 26: 1,074 lines out of an approximate total of 2,270.
June 27: 1,337 lines out of approximately 3,000.
June 28: 1,443 lines out of approximately 2,980.
June 29: 1,305 lines out of approximately 3,020.
June 30: 1,982 lines out of approximately 3,000.

Total during this week roughly 80,000 out of 160,000 words on Korea, or approximately 50 per cent of all news coverage during that week by the news section.

Finally, it should be pointed out that the desk output of that week as cited here represents only original broadcasts. It does not take into account the numerous repeats that are made at the transmitters, for instance, Munich, Salonika, Manila, etc., of original broadcasts.

PROPAGANDA TECHNIQUES IN USE AGAINST RUSSIA [11]

Listen to what the Voice is saying to the Russians and to the people in the satellite countries. It is tough talk:

The Russian people are oppressed by the Soviet government.

Stalin is a scheming, sly man, with all the attributes of a Hitler or a Mussolini.

Disaffection and restlessness are spreading through the Soviet Union and through her satellites like an indestructible fungus.

[11] From "One Voice That Stalin Hates," *Changing Times*, The Kiplinger Magazine. 5:24-28. May 1951. Reprinted by permission.

Exploitation of the Russian people gets worse with every passing day. The people cannot hope to improve themselves under their present regime.

The Russian talk of peace is phony. The Soviet leaders want war, because war is the way of all dictatorship.

The Kremlin has revived the Big Lie. The Kremlin discredits and distorts everything for its own ulterior purposes.

Imperialism is the keynote of Russian communism.

The United States wants peace and will stand by the United Nations. But it is all through being seduced by Soviet double talk and sugary promises. If necessary, the United States will fight.

Are these statements shockers? No more to you than to the Russian leaders. . . .

The Voice of America is a battery of radio transmitters ranging from 10,000 watts to 200,000 watts in power. It is also a staff of close to 2,000 people spotted all the way from New York to Honolulu to Salonika—the people who man the transmitters and speak the words. It is music and entertainment and news and commentary, but most of all it is propaganda. Don't forget that for a second. The Voice is just as much propaganda FOR us as the Russian press and radio are propaganda AGAINST us. . . . These broadcasts are dedicated to one purpose, and one purpose alone: the destruction of the Russian lie and the spread of the truth. Or, to put it in one-syllable words, the Voice is out to help us win. . . .

Some of the broadcasts go into the USSR seconds after they go on the air in New York. Others are picked up by the transmitting stations, put on phonograph records, and then broadcast and rebroadcast through the day and night without pause.

Sometimes the Voice teams up with the British Broadcasting Corporation's transmitters, and then the message is really pounded through. At such times 60 different transmitters broadcast the same voice and the same program. Imagine turning the dial on your own radio and getting the same program 60 different times, and you'll have some idea of the effect of this combination.

The building up of this powerhouse has taken millions of dollars. This fiscal year alone nearly $50 million was spent on new equipment for the broadcasters. The State Department hopes to spend an additional $100 million next year. If this is done, Russia will be "ringed." From every side her people will be bombarded with the Voice, bringing facts and the truth to people who have not had the truth for better than a quarter of a century, and for that matter, not much of the truth for several centuries before that.

In the beginning, we told the Russians little. We broadcast to them one hour out of 24, and it was pure guesswork as to whether anyone listened. The programs were harmless and folksy, loaded with good will and sentimental affection.

That was February 1947. Then, as United States policies toward Russia began to toughen, the programs toughened, too. For a while, the Soviets turned the other ear. They tried to ignore the broadcasts. Then Soviet journalist Ilya Ehrenburg blasted the Voice with all the vitriolic prose at his command, and the blast reverberated past the Urals. But the real payoff came on November 16, 1949, when Vishinsky stood up at the United Nations and acknowledged the Russians were at a war with us on the air waves. Russia had to block the programs, he said. If it didn't, the Russian people might "rise up in righteous indignation" against the Americans. His astounding, if unintentional, tribute was music to the ears of the Voice of America's mentors.

Today the programs follow a set pattern: news, editorial comment from United States papers, commentaries by special individuals, and such features as "U.N. Review," "Who Said It?" "Labor Roundup," "Interviews," "Life Behind the Iron Curtain," "Washington Observer," "Economic Roundup."

Everything is in Russian, spoken as the Russian speaks it. There is no music. No drama. No soap opera. No comedy. Time is too precious to waste on such things as these. Time is precious to the point where every minute counts, because the Russian who listens does so in a clandestine manner. There's not even a theme song or gong to identify the show (or betray the Russian listener whose radio is tuned in).

As to what the programs say, note these themes:

Quoting Lenin, the Voice recently said: "Comrade Stalin has concentrated an enormous power in his hands; and I am not sure he always knows how to use that power with sufficient caution. . . . Stalin is too rude. Therefore, I propose to the comrades to find a way to remove Stalin from that position and appoint another man . . . more patient, more loyal, more polite and more attentive to comrades." Such comments have been removed from Russian history books. The Voice is determined that the Russian people shall hear them.

The Voice likes to remind its listeners of Stalin's ruthlessness. "Wasn't it the leader's wisdom that ordered the liquidation of the kulaks?" it asks. "Isn't he the man who converted the Russian press into a phonograph record of a hymn of praise to one man?"

Then, in a different tone: "Are the peoples of Russia so devoid of talent, so lazy and so stupid that they could not dig canals, cut forests, dig coal or create an artistic life for themselves without a wise leader who stands by their side to inspire, guide and insist on every action?"

The Voice has labeled Stalin "Vozhd"—the Russian word for leader—and uses the word interchangeably with Duce or Führer. The Russian who listens begins, perhaps, to wonder about this man who has run his life for over 25 years. That is just what the Voice is after.

"The worker behind the Iron Curtain puts in a month's labor to get a suit; the American worker puts in a couple of days. United States incomes are at least five times as high as those in the USSR. When an American gets sick, his chances of getting a doctor are better than 10 to 1 over those of the Russian who gets sick. The Russian tax system is inequitable—it hits the poor. The Russian army system is inequitable—the captain gets 24 times the salary of the private."

Little things, little items, spread like scattershot by the Voice, planting doubts and resentments over an economic system that has been sold to its participants as the proletarians' paradise. The net effect: to undermine and weaken the authoritarian structure that Stalin has built.

There's an oil shortage in oil-rich Rumania, a coal shortage in coal-rich Poland, a food shortage in food-rich Hungary. Czechoslovakia is hungry because the Russians "forget" to send the grain they promised. Shoes are so scarce in Poland that a high-paid engineer has to work over two weeks to buy a single pair.

Why? The Voice states the fact, and leaves the question, "Why?" Does the Russian government grab everything? Is that where the food and oil go? Is the Communist speed-up nothing but the crack of the whip in the Kremlin? Those are the questions—and the answers that the Voice suggests.

And it goes further in the campaign to weaken Russia's hold on its satellites. It started a run on Rumanian banks by predicting a forthcoming devaluation of the Rumanian lei. At the same time an all-out hoarding spree broke out. By undivulged methods the Voice finds out what happens behind the Iron Curtain, and it reports the facts. Having heard, the people in the satellites move just an edge closer to dissatisfaction.

Slave labor is no fantasy. It is fact, the Voice tells the skeptical Russians. And to prove it is fact, it quotes such experts as Dr. Karl Garyk, former Czech official, who went on the air and reported that there are 30 to 40 major slave labor camps in his country, and 80 to 90 smaller camps, all of which hold 300,000 inmates. He located the camps and told how the inmates lived.

Another example: A prisoner's letter from the Black Sea Canal project was broadcast. It read: "We work voluntarily and only from 6 in the morning until 10 at night."

No slave labor behind the Iron Curtain? Any people who don't already know there is, will probably think differently when they hear the facts.

To the Russian claim that there are 18 million jobless in the United States, the Voice rejoins with a few facts. It reports the number of houses being built here. It tells of the 43 millon cars now on the road. It speaks of the giant labor unions, the 40-hour week, national minimum wage, unemployment insurance. It provides a little fresh air for a people who have been breathing the same stale air for a generation.

The Voice never attacks the Russian people. It never pokes fun at them or ridicules them. It speaks friendship and understanding and sympathy, and in doing this it encourages those tiny strains of discontent which can grow if properly nurtured.

It is pro-people, anti-regime. It doesn't demand sabotage or uprising, but it does nourish whatever hard core of resistance is left in the Russian folk.

It quotes Lincoln: "As I would not be a slave, so I would not be a master," and urges the Russian people to take heed. It quotes a letter from an Estonian widower who, after his wife died from lack of medical care, wrote: "The Soviet medical system has no heart." It quotes Ricardo Cocconi, Italian Communist leader who said, as he quit the party: "There was no discussion—only intimidation."

When a Soviet magazine, *Soviet Woman,* committed the unpardonable sin of publishing a picture of Stalin, Lenin AND Trotsky, the Voice remarked, "The fate of the editorial staff could not be immediately ascertained."

Little jokes are meat for the Voice. Typical was this one about "the pig maid Anna Rostova" who received "for her political consciousness and unquestionable cooperation, the highest award: a complete set of Stalin's works." "Serves her right," the Voice quoted an observer as saying.

PROPAGANDA TECHNIQUES: STRESSING RED DEFECTIONS [12]

The Voice of America, now that it is speaking up with some chance of being heard in Soviet Russia, is hammering hard on one of the best anti-Marxist themes in years: the widening Communist defections in Europe.

The story of bourgeois nationalist deviations, particularly in Italy, which the Voice is taking behind the Iron Curtain, comprises a skillful mixture of news and propaganda.

This impulse to blend news and propaganda, however, is not always lost when the Voice of America discusses America. As a consequence, the Voice sometimes takes on a tone that has a clear proadministration ring.

[12] From "Voice Now Stresses Widening Defections of Reds in Europe," by Robert W. Ruth, member, Washington bureau, *Baltimore Sun. Baltimore Sun.* p 1. February 16, 1951. Reprinted by permission. (Also in *Congressional Record.* 97: A1491-2. March 14, 1951.)

What the Voice tells the world is prepared here in the State Department's international broadcasting division. Last week a program entitled "Washington Observer" was teletyped to New York, where it was broadcast abroad in various languages. Its treatment of the congressional debate about how many troops to send to Europe went as follows:

> The so-called great debate on foreign affairs—that debate has left the fabric of the American foreign policy untorn. In fact, it turns out now that the process of discussion—as usual—is shaping a broader bipartisan platform.
>
> The issue . . . is not whether the President has the right to dispatch troops overseas. It is rather how much of a say Congress ought to be given in that decision. . . . Government and opposition apparently are coming closer together.

Then, in sharp contrast to widespread Republican views, the Voice went on:

> This narrowing of the issues debated tends to clear the political atmosphere. And at the same time defense problems have been clarified by General Eisenhower. His emphasis on the contagious interplay of courage—on Europe's need for equipment more than for troops—this prescription of Eisenhower's puts the defense problem on a new plane. Washington is almost unanimously agreed today that a great segment of public and congressional opinion is rallying on that plane.

Washington Observer told of rapid progress in strategic defense planning—tanks, planes, rifles, bombs, guns and ships being ordered at a rate of $3.5 billion a month and soon to be stepped up to $4 billion adding:

> From all that, a new feeling—a new sense is spreading in Washington. General Eisenhower is responsible for part, and at the end of the week, President Truman further swung Washington firmly into the lead.

Voice officials, however, contend that the Republican view is not ignored in its programs. They say that Senator Taft . . . and former President Hoover get their share of time in State Department broadcasts.

Less open to controversy are the Voice broadcasts on foreign affairs. Earlier this month the following program went out and much of it must have gotten to Moscow listeners because of the

Voice's recent success in outsmarting Soviet jamming transmitters:

> Last week two prominent Italian Communist deputies from Reggio Emilia resigned from the party. Since then there have been further resignations, and yesterday a strike set to take place in the area was called off by the Communists. The reason, according to press dispatches, is that they were afraid it would fail.
>
> The two men were Valdo Magnani and Aldo Cucchi. . . . Both enjoy great influence in Communist ranks. . . . The immediate cause of the resignations was a speech recently delivered by Magnani. He made it clear he still considers himself a good Communist. . . . What bothered him was the slavish way with which Communists follow the Moscow line. . . .
>
> The Italian Communist Party hierarchy was quick to sense the heresy of Magnani's remarks. . . . As a result, party circles in northern Italy are in a state of furor.

The Voice then took up another topic designed to salt Moscow wounds:

> Another personality is in the news, a prominent former Communist purged from his post on the charge of Titoism. The person is Vladimir Clementis, former Czechoslovak Foreign Minister. According to press dispatches, Mr. Clementis has fled from Prague. His whereabouts are a mystery. . . .
>
> Clementis was purged late last spring. The specific sin brought against him was that he had failed to accept the Nazi-Soviet pact of 1939; and that he had instead criticized it. According to his successor, Viliam Siroky, Clementis' crime was that he had lost his faith in Stalin.
>
> The connection between the purging of Clementis and last week's resignations of Italian Communists Magnani and Cucchi is obvious. All three, in Stalinist eyes, were guilty of the same sin: Of maintaining that a person can be a good Communist without accepting Soviet domination.

Although the Voice of America is rapidly maturing, it has yet to acquire much sex appeal—something which has great influence over Americans and Western Europeans. True, the Voice of America is sometimes the lush voice of Dinah Shore or Stafford, and sometimes Hollywood stars with foreign antecedents are worked into programs.

But the Voice feels compelled to be very proper in what it says to, say, French listeners, and suggestive noises are entirely taboo in programs beamed to the Middle and Far East for fear of offending oriental tastes.

Only disquieting whispers are directed to the ears of Mother Russia. After a long day's work in the fields, the Soviet woman is likely to get word via the Voice of America that the Communists lack the same enthusiasm for producing cosmetics that they do for hammers and sickles. If Mother Russia begins to feel like a drudge, a "gunny sack" (as one State Department official phrased it) and rises up and ousts her Communists oppressors, she can thank the Voice of America.

As for the Russian men the Voice never lets the Communists forget their setbacks in Western Germany—where they have lost elections, in France where their daily paper is losing circulation, in the Soviet zone of Austria where they get only five per cent of the votes, and in the rest of the Western world.

Other favorite topics: Russian slave labor, the Soviet-Chinese treaty, the adulation accorded Stalin in the Soviet press, the virtual banning of the literature of the great Russian writer, Fyodor Dostoyevsky, the Communist hate campaign against America, and the fate of a Chinese Communist basketball team which had been forced to lose to a Russian team.

PROPAGANDA TECHNIQUES: USING NURSERY STORIES[13]

Old Mother Goose has joined the "cold war" against the Soviet Union. The Voice of America is using nursery stories on its overseas propaganda broadcasts to kid Moscow's extravagant charges against the West. They try to expose by ridicule the upside-down arguments of Jacob Malik, Soviet delegate to the United Nations Security Council.

The Voice version of Mr. Malik says Cinderella was a victim of "craven monopolists," and what's more her case is on the agenda illegally. Mr. Malik is quoted as saying the sparrow that killed Cock Robin was just on a training mission, and was

[13] From "Mother Goose Joins 'Cold War' on Soviet," news story. New York *Times*. 99:53. September 24, 1950. Reprinted by permission.

not armed. The unfortunate fate of Little Red Riding Hood's grandmother—says "Malik"—cannot be discussed before the wolf is consulted.

This music-hall approach to propaganda is used in the Voice's "political cabaret" program. This broadcast is beamed to Eastern Europe where people are used to political farces on the stage. The Voice stories try to show that Mr. Malik's reports on international affairs are just as absurd as the upside-down nursery stories.

PROPAGANDA TECHNIQUES: USING MASS TRANSMISSION [14]

The Voice of America cleared its broadcast decks on April 14 for a mass transmission of an original one-hour radio version of the prize-winning Broadway play, *Darkness at Noon*. . . .

The program was beamed to Europe and the Near East from 2 to 3 P.M., EST, on 14 frequencies from the United States and relayed on five short-wave and one medium-wave frequency from Greece. Broadcasts ordinarily scheduled during that period in Serbo-Croat, Hungarian, Arabic, Bulgarian and Rumanian were canceled in order to utilize all available transmitting facilities for the antitotalitarian play.

The program was beamed to Latin America from 8 to 9 P.M, EST, on 16 frequencies and to the Far East from 8 to 9 A.M, EST, Sunday from Honolulu and three short-wave and one medium-wave frequency from Manila. The program was also repeated twice Sunday from relay bases at Tangier, Munich, and Salonika.

The English radio version was adapted from the Sidney Kingsley play which recently won the New York Drama Critics Award. . . . The play was based on Arthur Koestler's novel on the 1937 Moscow purge trials. . . .

[14] From "Mass Transmission of Drama 'Darkness at Noon' Over VOA," press release dated April 17, 1951. *Department of State Bulletin*. 24:700. April 30, 1951.

Later the voice of America plans to broadcast a score of foreign-language transmissions of *Darkness at Noon*, either in one-hour or in a series of shorter versions.

NEW ROLE OF EDUCATIONAL EXCHANGE IN PROPAGANDA [15]

As world conditions worsened, it became evident that although the objectives [of the educational exchange program] as originally conceived were still valid, they were inadequate and needed supplementation and sharpening. The Communist attack on the United States was not new, but the program as it was first conceived did not take into consideration intensive campaigns for the conversion of whole peoples to the Communist point of view. . . .

Major steps in this reshaping of the program may be cited as follows:

1. *Shaping the program to fit each country.* National attitudes and conditions in each country and area of the world have been analyzed from the standpoint of the objectives of the program to be conducted in each . . . to tailor the educational exchange program to fit the local situation.

2. *Sharpening the objectives of the program.* The aims of the educational exchange program have been examined and restated. Three specific objectives have been set up, the relative emphasis upon each being determined by conditions in the respective countries. In collaboration with the information program, the educational exchange service is now striving (a) to keep alive the spirit of cooperation among the free nations of the world for the purpose of self-protection and progress for all; (b) to strengthen resistance to communism in countries immediately threatened with infiltration or aggression; (c) to weaken the forces of communism and diminish its power in areas now under the domination of the USSR. . . .

[15] From "Educational Exchange Among Free Nations," fifth semiannual report to Congress of the United States Advisory Commission on Educational Exchange. *Department of State Bulletin.* 24:788-96. May 14, 1951.

3. *Review and redirection of specific program activities.* . . . An excellent illustration of this is the broadening function as well as the increase in the number of overseas libraries, now called United States information centers. In 1948 there were 67 overseas libraries and 22 reading rooms. By contrast, it is expected that the information centers will number 170 by June 30, 1951. Their change of name from libraries to information centers corresponds to the more positive role which has recently been assigned to them. In addition to providing books and other reference and extension services, they now arrange for lectures, discussion groups, and "workshops" for specialized groups such as teachers; show documentary films; and hold exhibits, as local conditions make these activities practicable and desirable. These information centers actively assist local institutions and groups along many lines, including the lending of materials to national libraries and educational institutions and providing English teaching materials and textbooks to local schools and groups.

The greatly expanded exchange-of-persons program is also being adapted to serve immediate needs more effectively. Grants formerly were limited chiefly to the academic and scientific fields. Exchange activities now include individuals in other representative categories: Government officials, labor groups, youth leaders, and professional leaders in all fields. There is an increased emphasis on bringing mature leaders and specialists to the United States on short-term visits. Even in student exchange, one of the main criteria in the selection of grantees is an individual's prospect of a position of influence in the near future.

A few statistics illustrate these new trends in the exchange of persons program, and also its expansion. In 1948 around 450 grants were awarded to students and adult professional leaders. In 1951, the plans provide for 1,555 grants from Smith-Mundt funds. With the addition of special educational exchange activities under the German program, the Fulbright Act, the Finnish program, and some others the total figure for 1951 is expected to exceed 6,500 grants. Roughly half of the 6,500 grants will be made to mature leaders selected from a number of representative fields for the purpose of lecturing, inspecting techniques, pursuing research projects, teaching, and other activities.

The Department of State's program, however, is only a small part of the total United States exchange-of-persons activities, the great bulk of which are carried out under private auspices in the United States and other countries. Over 30,000 foreign students are now studying on over a thousand American campuses. Not more than 9 or 10 per cent of these foreign students are supported by government grants. The great importance of this student migration and the teaching contribution of American educational institutions to an intellectually unified and cooperating world is impossible to calculate.

In some instances, the sharpening of the program to meet Communist attacks has been accomplished indirectly. For example, a number of appointments to qualified Negroes for study or other work abroad has done more to offset the charges of racial conflict in the United States than many articles on the subject could have done.

In a number of countries progress has been made to secure local support for the program. For example, binational American centers are being opened during the current fiscal year in Turkey, Iran, and Burma. These centers offer regular English classes, provide intensive English training for special groups such as educators, and offer courses and seminars on American civilization and other services.

Difference of language is always a barrier. . . . The Department of State is carrying out activities designed to increase the number of English-speaking peoples in various countries, as well as to reach other nationals through their own language by translating representative American publications.

English-teaching materials are being distributed to foreign schools and individuals engaged in the teaching of English. In addition, special English-teaching materials are being developed. These include textbooks and recordings in Korean, Vietnamese, Indonesian, Burmese, Turkish, and Persian. Experimentation is now under way to make effective use of motion pictures and radio as media for English teaching. Activities in the field of translation include financial and other assistance to foreign publishers for the translation and publication of American books, and government-financed translations of certain United States Government publications for distribution abroad. By the close of fiscal year 1951, nearly two million copies of translated American publications will have been distributed in 23 different languages.

FILMS IN PSYCHOLOGICAL WARFARE [16]

During the war, millimeter referred not only to the size of guns but also the gauge of a new weapon—the motion picture. Both 16mm. and 35mm. films were used extensively to help train the Armed Forces and war-production workers. Others helped to solidify the Allied nations and served as psychological weapons against the enemy. Today, along with press and radio, they are being used by the United States Information Service abroad to wage the peace.

Documentary and informational films depicting the American scene are reaching a foreign audience of approximately 100 million people annually. Within the last 24 hours films have gone out from 200 distribution points around the world for showing in countless cities, towns, and villages. . . .

The films used cover a wide cross section of our national life. They depict the daily lives of farmers and teachers, artisans and professionals. They describe our big industries and our small private businesses. Some present our great artists and musicians as well as museums. Others show the accomplishments of our people in the fields of science and education. They describe our great power projects and explain other activities of our federal, state, and local governments. Responsibilities assumed by the individual citizen in community affairs are indicated. They show people participating in local and national elections and taking active part in deciding other matters of public concern. They reflect the individual citizen's concern for his fellow man as demonstrated in ordinary neighborliness and in the work of our

[16] From "Films in the United States Information Program—The World Sees America," by Herbert T. Edwards. *Educational Screen.* 23:203-4. May 1949. Reprinted in *Congressional Record.* 96:A5553. July 20, 1950. Reprinted by permission.

great philanthropic organizations. Others explain our traditions and aspirations. These and other aspects of our national life constitute the subject-matter content of the films used. Together, they present the vast panorama of American life that this nation seeks to have understood abroad.

Showing these films is accomplished through a variety of arrangements. In all cases United States Information Service lends them free of charge to users. Many foreign posts are also able to supply operators and 16mm. projectors when film borrowers have no equipment or projectionist of their own. In addition, some mobile units are used. These travel to isolated communities in the interior and carry motor-driven generators for operating projection equipment in areas where there is no electric current.

While the USIS field staff frequently organizes its own showing, special effort is made to develop cooperative distribution projects with local groups and governments.

In Norway for instance, the labor party has found its members so interested in the United States that they prepare prints of USIS films at their own expense and distribute them for regular showings in over 50 labor halls. In some countries, as in Mexico and Egypt, these cooperative projects are on a national basis. Here the ministries of education, public health, and agriculture assume responsibility for the distribution and exhibition of USIS films throughout the country. In Mexico, that government defrays the entire cost of the showings, including the salaries of the operators, while the United States supplies the prints. Likewise, through official cooperation, these USIS films are exhibited throughout Egypt by agencies of that government. Arrangements similar to these have been developed in most of the American republics. . . .

Practically all films shipped abroad are 16mm. sound prints and scored in languages appropriate to the region served. As many as 24 different languages have been used in the past; however, budgetary limitations have made it necessary to reduce this to approximately 14 for films currently distributed.

Several projects are now being developed whereby major American industries can cooperate with the Department in the joint production of films with the sponsor using the picture domestically and the Department taking it for the overseas information program.

In addition to these activities, arrangements are made for the coverage of special events. Material of this type is furnished by the Department to the American newsreel companies and is included in their overseas editions.

Written materials and discussion guides are also prepared to accompany the principal documentary films. These materials supply information pertinent to the subject of the film and are made available to persons conducting the film showings in order that they can be conversant with topics directly related to the theme of the picture. Such supplementary information is helpful in leading discussions and answering questions. Incidentally, it is particularly useful in schools, where approximately 25 per cent of USIS showings are held. . . .

The use of motion pictures as part of the overseas information program is based on the premise that the evidence of the eyewitness is the most conclusive, that such evidence is as conclusive in human relations as in law, and that the sound motion picture is the nearest equivalent to direct observation and actual experience. The sound films are taking America to the millions who cannot actually visit this country. They are visualizing the American, his land, and his way of life, that the people of the world may see for themselves.

PROOF OF EFFECTIVENESS OF THE CAMPAIGN OF TRUTH

EDITOR'S INTRODUCTION

In the long run, the important thing to consider in psychological warfare is whether it is successful or not. The problems of providing any accurate measurement of success should be obvious, particularly with so many agencies involved and so many different audiences to consider. Complicating the situation was the limited budget for propaganda operations, which for all practical purposes made any reliable measurements of effectiveness impossible.

From a technical standpoint, much of the evidence of success in the propaganda war might legitimately be discounted. In the early years of the State Department's information program, "proof" of effectiveness was the total number of radio sets in a given country. In Congressional hearings concerned with appropriation of further funds for information activities, Department spokesmen presented elaborate charts showing the number of people per country, the number of radio sets, the number of sets with short-wave bands, and some rather arbitrary estimates of total listeners derived by multiplying an estimate of "listeners per set" by the total sets in the country. Listenership to the Voice of America, according to this device, was phenomenal, but the method of measurement was wholly contradictory to everything developed over a period of years in domestic radio research. Later, and even now to a large extent, audience mail was the chief guide to listening to the Voice of America. This too cannot be considered too reliable, if domestic radio experience with audience mail is any guide. There is no way of knowing whether the people who write letters to the Voice of America are the majority of the people who listen, or only a small proportion. Presumably they represent only a small percentage, but there is no sure way of telling on the basis of the mail itself.

But the Department of State recognizes the problem and has greatly expanded its Program Evaluation Branch of the Office of International Information to provide a more accurate guide to effectiveness of the program. Audience surveys are being conducted to a limited extent, but they are tremendously expensive when conducted on a global scale. Also, it would be exceedingly difficult to conduct a survey behind the Iron Curtain where admission of listening to foreign broadcasts is punishable by fine or imprisonment.

Both as a guide in planning Voice of America broadcasts and in determining probable effects of such broadcasts, listener panels are being employed extensively, in Europe at least. These panels, made up presumably of natives of the country and representing various shades of opinion and all walks of life, review Voice programs and offer criticisms and suggestions for improvement. The extent to which this device is employed is not known, nor is it known how accurate a guide to ultimate effectiveness such a technique might be.

In general, this chapter attempts to present those proofs of effectiveness which have some basis of documentary evidence, not merely individual opinions.

SUMMARY OF EFFECTIVENESS OF THE VOICE[1]

We are presently broadcasting over a worldwide network of transmitter bases in 33 languages. We operate around the clock, sending out in these languages more than 80 separate programs a day, each tailored specifically for the time of day and the attitudes of the target audiences. We process over 2 million words daily and put more than 350,000 out over the air waves. We are expanding even from these staggering figures. Within a few months we expect to be using 50 languages and broadcasting over a hundred programs daily, about 60 hours of "live" programs, containing over a half million words. The United States taxpayer has an investment in facilities already operating or under construction of about $125 million. . . . If Congress approves, this will be increased by an additional hundred million within the next couple of years. The cost of programming and operating is presently running at the rate of approximately $25 million per annum and if the new facilities are granted will gradually work up to a high level of about $45 million per year.

Is the taxpayer getting his money's worth? Is the Voice of America effective? . . . The question of effectiveness of the Voice of America, as I see it, involves really three questions: (1) Are we delivering a clear, strong signal? (2) Are we getting an audience? Indeed, do the possibilities of getting an audience exist? (3) Are we affecting the minds and influencing the actions of our audience in a sense favorable to the interests and

[1] From "Effectiveness of the Voice of America," address by Foy D. Kohler, Chief, International Broadcasting Division, before the Institute for Education by Radio-Television, Columbus, Ohio, May 4, 1951.

aspirations of the American Government and the American people?

I can deal with the first two questions only in passing. With respect to the first, "Are we delivering a clear strong signal?" The United States is severely handicapped in international broadcasting by its geographic location. Shortwave radio is, in any event, a medium with severe limitations both in terms of the quality of the signal and of access to the signal by prospective listeners. To overcome these handicaps we have started to ring the world with relay bases which boost the signal to the listeners via both short and medium wave. We are developing overseas program operations. We are doing our best to obtain local relays wherever there is such a possibility. We are pioneering in advanced techniques and superpower, with the collaboration of the best electronic engineering groups in the country. If Congress gives us the necessary financial support, we can deliver an effective radio signal, even through the Soviet jamming.

With respect to the second element, "Are we getting an audience?" We are extremely fortunate in that radio, even in relatively backward areas of the world, is an established and fairly highly developed medium of communication. We have available either firm figures or solid estimates on the number of radio receivers which we can reach throughout the world. We know there are about 80 million receiving sets outside of North America, giving international broadcasters a direct potential audience of over 300 million people, not to mention secondary distribution. And we are able, at comparatively low cost, to promote ever-wider distribution of receivers. Within the free world we can apply, with some adaptation, the techniques of quantitative audience surveys so highly developed in the United States. Through these we are able to get an accurate measure of the size, composition and other characteristics of our audience and of changes in these elements. To do this we use mainly private contractors, notably such organizations as the American Institute of Public Opinion (Gallup Polls) and its overseas affiliates; and the Bureau of Applied Social Research of Columbia University (Kingsley Davis-Paul Lazarsfeld).

I can give you only a few examples of our findings. We thus know that in France, where our program is rebroadcast over the French domestic network, our audience has increased constantly and greatly in size during the past few years. We know that over 24 per cent of the adult population of France—7 million people—are at least occasional listeners to the Voice programs, that on any given weekday we can count on an audience of at least a million people and that we have nearly 3 million on Sundays. We know that over half the adult population of that country has heard the Voice of America at some time, and that our problem is to get more and more of them tuning in regularly. We know that this audience includes the better educated and urban residents in greater proportion than their ratio to the total population.

In Germany we know that we have likewise been able to bring more and more Germans to their receivers when we are on the air; that we now have a regular audience numbering over 6 million in the United States Zone alone. Here the audience is characterized by its proportionate accent on youth—a very good thing, I would say.

In Sweden surveys indicate an occasional audience for our English-language broadcast of 15 per cent of the total Swedish population, or over 700,000 people and a regular audience of nearly 100,000, heavily weighted on the side of so-called "opinion leaders" and of youth. The same studies, based on direct sampling and on analysis of BBC's Swedish audience, made it clear that we could multiply our audience many-fold and get their more consistent attention to our story if we broadcast in the Swedish language. We are, accordingly, preparing to do so during the coming fiscal year.

You will recognize that I have been talking about relatively advanced and accessible areas. Unfortunately the job is a lot harder outside Western Europe. . . .

Behind the curtain, in the satellite states of Eastern Europe we have of course been unable to make direct surveys. However, we are not without our resources here either. We have firm figures from pre-slavery days on the distribution of radio sets and sufficient current intelligence to keep these up to date.

Research agencies, letters from displaced persons, interrogation of defectors, United States Missions—all these sources are surprisingly unanimous in agreeing that we reach about 80 per cent of the radio owners every day, and that the Voice of America, with the assistance of the well-developed grapevine, can deliver an important message to practically the entire population of the satellite states within a matter of hours. Similar sources indicate that there has been a comparably sharpened interest in China since the Communists took over. The frantic efforts of local stooge governments to combat our efforts confirm these estimates.

In the Soviet Union, in the early days of our Russian-language program, which was inaugurated in February 1947, all the evidence we could amass at the Embassy in Moscow indicated that the Voice of America must have a regular listening audience of at least 10 million people. What the figure is since the Kremlin indicated its disapproval of listening, by undertaking a colossal jamming campaign in April 1949, nobody really could know. However, our monitoring indicates that we have greatly improved the delivery of our signal since that date; that the Voice can be heard 25 per cent of the time even in Moscow, where the jamming is concentrated, and 60 to 80 per cent of the time outside the capital. Moreover, defectors continue to give us a pattern of widespread listening and the Soviet press and radio contribute additional evidence. . . .

So much for audience measurement. Now, what is the Voice's impact on the audiences we reach? This question involves even more intangibles in the international field than in the field of domestic radio. . . . It involves questions of the analysis of the content of our programs and their measurement against our communications intentions. It involves ascertaining sample audiences' reaction to specific programs through the panel technique and the use of such devices as the Stanton-Lazarsfeld reaction analyzer. It involves the testing of the level and quality of the language we use in our 30-odd language programs and audience reaction to specific announcers' voices and method of delivery. For all these purposes we can also use established American methods and techniques and the services of objective and experienced American research agencies like International Public

Opinion Research, Inc. (Elmo Wilson, Elmo Roper, Joshua Powers), McCann Erickson, The Committee on Communications of the University of Chicago, and the Research Study for Human Relations of New York University. Within the free world tests can be made on the spot in the target countries. For testing programs delivered behind the Iron Curtain, panels of recent defectors are assembled both along the immediate periphery of the Soviet orbit and here in the United States. . . .

In a general way . . . I think it is clear that the Voice of America can take a considerable share of the credit for fostering the growing strength and determination of the free world; for the succession of 50-odd to 5 votes in the United Nations condemning Communist aggression in Korea; for the declining strength of communism throughout the free world, and particularly in such vital countries as France and Italy.

This is attested by the constantly increasing size and interest of our free world audience, of which I have spoken. It is reflected in ever-growing demands for our program schedule booklet. This schedule is sent to listeners on written request only, and circulation figures have mounted in the past year from 500,000 to nearly 900,000 copies per issue. General effectiveness is also shown by the steady upward trend of our audience mail. In 1949 we received 126,000 letters from our listeners; in 1950 230,000. In March of this year we reached an all-time high of nearly 40,000 letters for one month alone.

Now I realize that these booklets and letters are not scientifically established methods of measurement comparable to our surveys and panel tests, but they are very heartwarming and encouraging. And they do give us valid and sometimes striking examples of audience attitudes and changes therein. . . . Occasionally we have striking demonstrations of our direct influence, such as that of the two Soviet aviators who flew their plane straight out of the Soviet Union a couple of years ago. The unabated efforts of the Kremlin to keep our message out of the Soviet Union by the use of their colossal jamming network is another measure of the Kremlin's own estimate of our effectiveness with the Soviet citizenry. Even better is the constant stream of attacks made on us over the Soviet radio and in the Soviet press. These have gone from a quarterly level of 30-odd full-dress attacks in 1949 to over 100 during the last quarter of 1950. They are so voluminous and so revealing that we have them under constant analysis by the Russian Research Center at Harvard University. Not only do they give us a concept of the extent and composition of our audience, as I have already suggested, but they indicate the themes to which the Kremlin is particularly sensitive and which it feels compelled to try to rebut. . . .

BACKGROUND OF "JAMMING" VOA BROADCASTS [2]

For months newspapers throughout the country headlined the Russian "jamming" of Voice of America broadcasts directed toward the Soviet Union. These dramatic stories of a tremendous radio battle, with the United States and United Kingdom on one side and the Soviets on the other, highlight the role broadcasting is playing in the ideological war between the free and the slave states. It is an excellent example of radio as an instrument of political warfare.

Actually, the air war is not a novel development; the Russians have been jamming the Voice of America and the BBC since early in 1948. . . . In a speech to the High Frequency Broadcasting Conference at Mexico City on April 8, 1949, the Chairman of the United States delegation delivered a scathing indictment of the Russians for the jamming which the Soviets had been doing at the very times when its delegations to international broadcasting conferences were imploring the conferees to "cooperate" and to join with the Soviet Union in developing frequency assignment plans.

Shortly after this speech, the Soviet Union intensified its interference activities noticeably. Then, when the story of the lifting of the Berlin blockade was announced, and the voices of the free peoples of the West began to report the truth to the oppressed peoples behind the Iron Curtain, the Soviet Union intensified its jamming activities to an incredible extent.

[2] From "That People May Speak Unto People," by Forney A. Rankin, public affairs advisor to the Assistant Secretary of State for Inter-American Affairs, Department of State. *World Affairs.* 113:38. Summer 1950. Reprinted by permission.

METHODS AND MEANINGS IN THE JAMMING AIR WAR [3]

Short of destroying the transmitters, there is only one way the Russians can block the Voice's signal. That is to jam it. Jamming produces roughly the same thing as tuning in two radio stations at once. You know how annoying that can be. Think how annoying it would be if you were tuned in to a program and it was suddenly blotted out by the roar of a motor, the hum of a vacuum cleaner, the clash of grinding gears, the high shriek of a sea gull, the roar of a lion, the blood-curdling wail of a banshee, the grind-grind-grind of a buzz saw. It takes a sharp and patient ear to listen to any program above the racket of a jammer.

Jamming can be done in several ways. One is by electronic jamming—in other words, man-made static. Another is by playing over and over again phonograph records of such sounds as those listed above.

The Russians have as many as 1,000 radio stations which do nothing but jam the Voice of America. Some are "sky wave" jammers—Big Berthas which can knock out programs over an area of thousands of square miles. Others are "ground wave" jammers—designed to block programs in individual cities and towns. Thousands of technicians man these stations. They are the Voice's enemy in the line.

The big jam started April 24, 1949. The Russians "got" everything, and if the Voice shifted from one wave length to another, the jammers were on top of it in a matter of seconds.

It took weeks and months of planning and building, but the Voice people now think the jam is licked, at least part way. About 25 per cent of all programs beamed from here reach Russian listeners in Moscow. Outside of Moscow the percentage is estimated to be three times that much.

Various tricks—some known, some secret—are tried in this counterjam. For one thing, special antennas are used to concen-

[3] From "One Voice That Stalin Hates." *Changing Times,* The Kiplinger Magazine. 5:24-8. May 1951. Reprinted by permission.

trate the Voice's strength. For another, big, powerful new stations are being built to outshoot the jammers. "Cuddling" is the most effective method of getting the jammers. Cuddling is the technique of broadcasting the Voice's programs on a wave length right next to the Soviets' own programs. This accomplishes two things: (1) It enables the secret listener to shift his dial back and forth from a Russian program to a United States program without easy detection; (2) it forces the Russians to block out their own programs if they want to "get" ours. The Russians often keep jamming anyhow.

EVIDENCE OF SUCCESS IN EVADING SOVIET JAMMING [4]

Soviet jamming of Voice of America broadcasts is relatively ineffective in many areas of the Soviet Union and well over half the Voice's output can be heard clearly in many regions, authenticated reports from the Soviet Union reveal. It is known that standard Soviet radios at widely separated points in the Soviet Union can receive most of the Voice's output without serious distortion.

Before receipt of these reports, information coming from Moscow and Leningrad had indicated that only about 20 per cent of the Voice's broadcasts could penetrate the barrier set up by Soviet jamming stations. The new information, from a number of major provincial centers, indicates that the effectiveness of this jamming is at a peak near Moscow and Leningrad where the interfering stations apparently have their greatest concentration.

Elsewhere over the wide expanse of the Soviet Union, the evidence indicates, jamming stations are spread more thinly and are correspondingly less effective. Even in Moscow and Leningrad, the effectiveness of the interference efforts varies

[4] From "More 'Voice' News Reaching Russians," by Harry Schwartz, Associate Professor of Economics, Syracuse University, and specialist on Russian affairs for the New York *Times*. New York *Times*. 100:3. February 16, 1951. Reprinted by permission.

greatly from time to time, depending upon climatic conditions and the season of the year, so that there have been periods when far more than 20 per cent of the broadcasts could be heard clearly.

Additional evidence that Voice transmissions are reaching a significant fraction of Soviet people seems provided by a study of Soviet press and radio reaction to the Voice of America conducted at Harvard University under the supervision of Professor Alex Inkeles.

This study, covering the period from March 1, 1947, to September 30, 1950, found a sharply upward trend during the last two years in the number of press and radio references to and attacks upon the Voice. From March 1, 1947, to July 31, 1949, such references averaged 30 during each three-month period. From July 1, 1950, to September 30, 1950, however, there were 99 such references, of which 29 were concerned with the Soviet anti-American play, "Voice of America." If repeat broadcasts are included, the number of references rises to 178.

During July to September of last year, the Voice of America was the primary or a major focus of attack 16 times in 8 mass-circulation Soviet newspapers and magazines. The Voice of America was attacked by Soviet radio broadcasts 102 times during these same three months. The great bulk of these efforts, however, were aimed at audiences outside the Soviet Union, particularly those in Eastern and Western Europe.

Professor Inkeles' study found that much of the anti-Voice of America propaganda assumed that the Soviet audience knew what the Voice was, and even hinted at times that large numbers listened to the American broadcasts.

MAIL RESPONSE TO THE VOICE [5]

Listener mail in February 1951 reached a total of 30,397 letters, second in volume only to the record month of December

[5] From *Report on Audience Mail February 1951*, Program Evaluation Branch, International Broadcasting Division, Office of International Information, Department of State. (Report #AM-30) p 1-3.

1950, when 34,763 letters were received. (The total for March was . . . 39,741 letters.)

It is significant to note that the large February total was achieved without the stimulus of any major broadcast offers, such as the announcement of the availability of the "Outline of American History" publication, which accounted for 10,671 letters from Austria in December 1950. Requests for promotional materials (other than the program schedule) in all major languages in February totaled 3,711 as compared with 13,886 in December.

The outstanding development in February mail was the response to the offer of program schedules in programs to Yugoslavia, inaugurated on February 1 and continued daily throughout the month. Yugoslav (Slovenian and Serbo-Croat) mail in February reached a total of 1,212 letters, as compared with 338 for all of 1949 and 1950 combined.

A sharp rise in mail from certain areas in February is discernible. Mail from Germany, always one of the principal sources of listener reaction, averaged 6,649 per month in 1950; the mail from Germany in February 1951 was 11,015. This may be partially explained by the effect of regular announcements of the program schedule, which had been offered only sporadically in late 1950. In February, 82 per cent of the German mail consisted exclusively of program schedule requests.

Mail from Italy also shows a substantial increase from a monthly average of 1,968 in 1950 to a February total of 2,927. A considerable portion of this increase is attributed to a greater interest in receiving copies of broadcast scripts. Requests for such material averaged 800 a month in 1950 as compared with 1,794 in February 1951.

Turkish mail in February reached an all-time high of 1,785 letters, as compared with a monthly average of 462 in 1950. The broadcast offer of copies of the scripts of the program called "Epic of Korea," dealing with the Turkish Army, accounted for 446 letters in February, of which 366 were devoted exclusively to requests for the script.

POPULARITY OF VOA PROGRAMS: GERMANY [6]

The majority of United States Zone and Western Berlin residents interviewed in a poll of current attitudes regarding the Voice broadcasts described the programs as "good" because they were informative and instructive.

The poll, completed by the Reactions Analysis staff of the Office of Public Affairs, HICOG, in which trained German interviewers made a representative sampling of opinion of 3,000 in the zone, 500 in Berlin and 300 in Bremen, also disclosed that the Voice of America audience in Western Berlin had increased by 17 per cent since June 1949 when a similar study was made. This audience is now estimated at 55 per cent of the population of Western Berlin.

In the United States Zone, there has been little change in the size of the audience. Of those polled, 36 per cent said they generally listen to the broadcasts which are especially tailored for German audiences and beamed direct from New York for relay by Radio Bremen, Radio Frankfurt, Radio Munich, Radio Stuttgart and RIAS in Berlin. Listenership in all places surveyed was 39 per cent of the total public, and 60 per cent of German radio listeners.

WHAT LISTENERS SAY ABOUT THE VOICE [7]

I would like to stress the fact that your broadcasts are clearly heard; your programs have such variety that through them we learn all about the political events in the world and about social life in the USA. . . . My husband and I regularly listen to the Serbo-Croat and Hungarian broadcasts of the Voice of

[6] From " 'Voice of America' Programs Rated Good," news story. *Information Bulletin* (of the Office of the United States High Commissioner for Germany). p 11. October 1950.

[7] From *Report on Audience Mail February 1951,* Program Evaluation Branch, International Broadcasting Division, Office of International Information, Department of State. (Report #AM-30). p 12-22.

America. I am Hungarian and my husband is a Serb.——Zrenjanin, Yugoslavia—February 10, 1951.

I have always wanted to tell you how I enjoy your programs (I mean the Voice of America programs), how interesting and informative they are. . . . Your special tributary program on the 30th of January 1951, on the third anniversary of Mahatma Gandhi's martyrdom was the most exciting program I ever heard over the radio. I take this opportunity to congratulate you on your excellent presentment, clear enunciation and perfect diction. Those who want an impartial criticism on day-to-day world affairs have the most enchanting and truthful commentator, "The Voice of America."——Kumbakonam, S. India—February 12, 1951.

I have been listening to the VOA programs for over a year now and I have a great deal of admiration for them. My work schedule does not permit me to listen to the majority of your broadcasts, but I rarely miss *Panorami d'America* which I feel is one of your most interesting and well-planned programs——Genova, Italy—January 13, 1951.

The half hour Turkish program of the VOA fosters 100 per cent Turco-American friendship.——Turgutlu, Turkey—January 25, 1951.

Today I would like to thank you for your marvelous broadcasts. I am from the Eastern Zone and I can tell you that you and RIAS are the only consolation we still have. Actually all listeners of the Voice and of RIAS should be organized.——Burgau, Germany—February 10, 1951.

The undersigned, enthusiastic listener of the Voice of America, is very grateful to all our American friends for the truly and very detailed information about all the events throughout the wide world in all national languages. I think that the most powerful weapon, the TRUTH, and the most aimed goal, the FREEDOM, are well represented in the Voice of America.——Split, Yugoslavia—February 4, 1951.

Today, in these difficult days, the whole free world is looking up at the US. For this confidence which the world has in the US, you are (Voice of America) partly responsible, because in your programs you gave us real interviews with American workers, about their life and standard of living——Yugoslavia—February 10, 1951.

In this city, and possibly throughout Spain, more and more people talk about your broadcasts, and the number of listeners is always increasing. My explanation of this phenomenon is that the VOA's commentaries are the clearest and most unbiased, sometimes bordering upon what may be termed crude frankness, thereby winning the confidence of its audience.——Orense, Spain—January 20, 1951.

Radio is the only medium on which the humble classes rely for information and knowledge of the great North American nation, a country that is so much admired throughout the world. The VOA should, in all fairness, feel very proud of its achievements and contribution toward this end——Reus, Spain—December 28, 1950.

A TURKISH VIEW OF TRUTH STRATEGY [8]

Moscow propaganda long has applied the big-lie technique, developed by Adolf Hitler, in its attacks upon the free nations of the world. The United States Government, in its information output, has sought to counter the big lie by sticking to factual reporting. This policy is based on the conviction that, in the long run, the truth will prevail.

A recent telegram from the United States Embassy in Ankara, Turkey, is indicative of the success of this policy. The telegram reported that the cultural attaché of the Embassy, in a recent visit to the town of Bolu, in northwest Turkey, asked Presat Aker, former mayor and a respected elder of the community, whether the villagers listened to the Voice of America. He replied:

> Yes, indeed. We advise those among us who have radios to listen to the Voice of America if they would hear the truth. Some of us listen to Moscow radio too, so we can tell our people how the Russians are

[8] From "Soviet Big Lie *vs.* the Campaign of Truth," press release dated April 3, 1951. *Department of State Bulletin.* 24:639. April 16, 1951.

lying. The people have been aware of Radio Moscow's tactics ever since it reported the entire Turkish brigade in Korea had been wiped out, including General Yazici. When letters kept coming from friends in Korea, our people knew the Russians were lying. We tell them the Voice of America tells the truth about the Korean war, including accurate casualty figures, and that they can believe it.

POTENCY OF OVERSEAS INFORMATION CENTERS [9]

"Few of us can visit America," writes a research chemist in Spain, "and, except for the books from the United States Information Center, we have practically no contact with American science and technology."

Similar comments are received almost continuously by the 140 United States Information Centers maintained by the Department of State in 62 countries, exclusive of 21 Centers closed since July 1949 because of Communist opposition in Bulgaria, China, Czechoslovakia, Korea, and Russia. . . .

In 1950, approximately 24 million foreign nationals used the books and other facilities of these centers. A very large proportion of these patrons were national leaders—public officials, doctors, lawyers, business men, educators, architects, newspapermen, and others—seeking information for use in their day to day work. Many were persons engaged in long-range programs designed to increase national productivity and raise standards of living within their home countries. In connection with such programs, the United States Information Centers are playing an important role, in furnishing the books and other information concerning United States experience in similar programs.

Of the many important projects in other countries which have been and are being assisted by materials supplied by United States Information Centers, a few typical examples are as follows:

[9] From "United States Information Centers Overseas," by Lawrence S. Morris, chief, Division of Libraries and Institutes, United States Department of State. Institute of International Education *News Bulletin*. 26:7-9. March 1, 1951. Reprinted by permission.

In Western Germany, the United States Information Centers are a potent force in the vast campaign of reorientation of the German people toward Western democracy. According to Dr. Theodore Huebener, of the Board of Education of the City of New York, who recently returned from a tour of duty in Germany as a special consultant of the State Department, the Centers are "by far the most important and most effective organization in the entire scheme of reorientation." This, he points out, is due to the fact that each center is a permanent institution, that it has the closest personal relationships with the community, and that its programs are varied, including library services, lectures, discussions, films, music, exhibits, and children's activities.

Activities of the Center libraries include reference services given to newspapers, theaters, city health departments, libraries, prison officials, and farmers. Information Centers are maintained in all the leading university cities in the United States Zone, and in Hamburg, Hannover, and Essen in the British Zone, and are constantly used by professors, teachers, and students. The open shelf system of the Information Center libraries has so favorably impressed German patrons that in several instances they have requested that their public libraries change to open shelves.

An exhibit of the American Institute of Architects (originally prepared for the Pan-American Congress of Architects in Havana) which is being circulated under Information Center auspices among the largest cities in Germany is regarded as "probably the contribution of greatest significance for architecture and city planning in Germany," according to Hugo Leipziger-Pearce in the *Journal of the AIA.*

During the period when the Government of India was organizing its executive, legislative, and judicial departments and drafting its constitution, officials of the various ministries of the government and of the Constituent Assembly constantly turned to the United States Information Center library of New Delhi for publications to assist them in their work.

The Indian Government continues to use the library for information covering a variety of fields. Officials of the health department are using publications from the Center on housing administration, slum clearance, housing on a cooperative basis, and government and private health projects. The India Institute of Accounting and Taxation has been using information, supplied by the Center, on how the United States handles such problems as tax evasion, limit of taxation for industrial advancement, auditing and accounting for business. The development of river projects in India has brought many inquiries concerning American experience with similar projects, such as TVA and Boulder Dam; the Center has provided a quantity of material which is being used by officials of the Damodar Valley Corporation, as well as officials of the government of Orissa and West Bengal.

The new Constitution of Burma was written almost single-handedly by U Chan Htoon, now Attorney General of Burma, aided by books and documents on the Constitution of the United States which he obtained from the United States Information Center. The report of the Hoover Commission on Reorganization was used by a committee working on the reorganization of the Government of Burma. Books on forestry provided to the principal forest officer of the Shan States, and the book, *The TVA Lessons for International Application*, are being used in developing plans for the rehabilitation of the Shan States. The reforestation program of southern France is also being aided by books supplied by the United States Information Center at Bordeaux.

In Denmark, the State Teachers College is offering its first course in American history, aided by textbooks and maps borrowed from the Center at Copenhagen. Danish editors revising English-language readers for Denmark's schools obtained from the same Center selections from American literature to be included for the first time in the readers.

The University of Seville has established its first general course on the United States, emphasizing American history and foreign policy, for which the United States Information Center at Madrid is providing appropriate reading materials.

In Manila, the home weaving industry may be improved by a new type of loom for local weavers which has been made by the Loom Shop Superintendent of the Philippine Relief and Trade Rehabilitation Administration (PRATRA); the Information Center supplied the book, *Foot-Power Loom Weaving*, by Worst, which suggested the design. Blue prints of the model will be distributed throughout the Islands by PRATRA. The Manila City Councilor, with the help of materials on housing from the Information Center, prepared and secured passage of a municipal law setting up a Housing Board.

These are only a few examples which indicate that the Information Centers fill a deep cultural and intellectual need in all parts of the world. Unquestionably their influence penetrates deeply into the lives of many millions of people, by whom they are regarded as America's best ambassadors of good will.

FIELD REPORTS OF EFFECTIVENESS OF FILMS [10]

[Extracts from field reports of the United States Information and Educational Exchange film program]

Greece, November 1949: Showings of USIE films to Communist prisoners continue at the political reorientation camp on the Makronessos Islands. At this camp one of the most unique experiments in the modern political world is taking place. USIE films form a regular part of the reeducation program for Communists being detained there. Greek Army officers working on the project express warm appreciation for the films and confidence in their effectiveness.

Chile, December 1949: Once again this year, USIE films were the basis for annual semester projects in the local schools. Students constructed models of things seen in USIE films and these were presented in a citywide exhibition. Sixty thousand students from 160 local schools participated in the exhibition.

Denmark, May 1950: In order to reach key groups USIE has concentrated on multiple film showings to small groups with specific interests. As a result of this policy, more than 600

[10] From field reports of the USIE film program. *Congressional Record.* 96: A5552. July 20, 1950.

showings take place each month. In Copenhagen alone, the film section frequently arranges showings by each of six projectionists on the same evening. Responsible officers state that the film section has accomplished near miracles with the equipment available and request the allocation of additional equipment.

Indonesia, April 1950: Reports indicate that many people walk 10 kilometers to see USIE film showings and that even heavy rains fail to keep the people away.

Finland, February 1950: On numerous occasions when projectors are sent to outlying districts, this office is amazed at the considerable use they are given. A high school teacher in one town borrowed a projector and several films for three days. During that time she gave 10 different performances to 2,735 persons.

Italy, March 1950: When USIE advertised a film showing in a small town near Florence, the local Communist Party immediately announced the showing of a Sovexport film at the same time. When the showings were held 250 spectators came to the USIE show while 15 attended the Communist exhibition. It was later discovered that many who attended the USIE show had contributed to the rental of the Soviet picture.

Mexico, May 1950: An ambitious and carefully planned mobile unit tour was undertaken in the State of Hidalgo to continue from March 9 to April 23 covering 1,800 miles. The tour was conducted in close cooperation with state and community officials and in the company of local agricultural, educational, and health officers. The mobile unit visited 45 towns and showed films to at least 60,000 persons. Everywhere Embassy representatives were cordially received by the people, labor union and civic leaders, as well as all local authorities. The good will engendered is hard to visualize for persons who have not experienced similar occasions in Mexico.

The Embassy has received invitations from the governors of two other states to arrange similar mobile unit tours.

Philippines, April 1950: The USIE-Davao mobile unit reached an audience of over 82,000 persons during a 23-day tour of the Island of Mindanao. Despite the prevalent unrest throughout the countryside, the unit was warmly welcomed everywhere it went.

EVIDENCE OF COMMUNIST SETBACKS [11]

Who said that we are losing the so-called cold war? Certainly not the Russians! On the contrary, they are right now accusing us of such successes that they are trying to persuade the peoples of Europe that their governments have sold out to us. . . .

Let's take the case of France, where we can see that the Communist Party has suffered successive and continual losses in prestige and effectiveness since 1947. In 1949-1950, the Communists were unable to touch off a strike of any real importance. They have lost two thirds of the members in the Communist-dominated federation in spite of constant agitation. The Communists flopped in their strenuous efforts to persuade the French people to reject the North Atlantic Treaty and the Mutual Defense Assistance Program. . . . The circulation of their leading newspaper has dropped in the last five years from 500,000 to just over 200,000. . . . The Communist vote has declined in elections throughout Europe. Even in Austria, one third still under the Soviet army's heel, the voters have turned out Communist officials. The defection of key Communist leaders in Italy is significant. . . .

In the Far East, the picture, of course, is less rosy. . . . But we have multiple indications that the low point has been reached and that the tide has probably turned. . . . The unbelievably vicious Hate-America campaign which has been conducted in China for three months has proved disappointing to the Communists. And, as stooge Chinese troops are paying an increasingly dreadful price for their aggression in Korea, the first signs of unrest in this adventure are beginning to show on the Chinese home front. I don't mean to imply that a revolt in China is in the offing—or anything like it. I do mean to imply that, from a low point, the tide seems to have turned in much of the Far East.

[11] From "The Turn of the Tide," by Edward W. Barrett, Assistant Secretary for Public Affairs. *Department of State Bulletin.* 24:352-4. February 26, 1951.

Now, mind you, I don't say all this is by any means attributable to the accomplishment of the government's Campaign of Truth. Propaganda—particularly our propaganda of truth—depends on action. The actions of the nations of the free world have paved the way. The Marshall Plan has played a great role. General Eisenhower is a major factor in Europe. Our toughness against great odds in Korea has heralded to the world that aggressors will pay a stupendous toll. And the Soviet rulers themselves, by their own crass and often blundering propaganda, have contributed to their own declining influences. . . .

I do say that this government's Campaign of Truth, together with the smaller information services of other governments and various private media, have played a great role in blazoning these truths to the world. And, accordingly, the big lie is losing ground, rapidly in some areas, before the new truth offensive of the free world.

CRITICAL EVALUATIONS OF THE PROPAGANDA EFFORT

EDITOR'S INTRODUCTION

As might be expected with a program that has increased ten-fold in a short time, the stepped-up Campaign of Truth has met with serious criticism. While critics of the sykewar operation tend to be more newsworthy than the defenders of the program, much of the criticism has been evaluative in nature and apparently sincere. Certainly it has been voluminous enough, covering almost every aspect of the propaganda effect from personnel to strategy.

Perhaps the most authoritative evaluations of the current program are those of the Advisory Commissions set up under the Smith-Mundt Act to oversee the information and educational exchange operations. These commissions are composed of outstanding specialists in their respective fields and report semi-annually to Congress on the accomplishments of the program under their jurisdiction. Since the government information program is the chief agency of the propaganda effort, it naturally has been the subject of most of the attacks. Consequently, the Advisory Commission on Information recently recommended the formation of a number of supplementary committees to deal with various aspects of the information program such as motion pictures, audience measurement, radio, etc. These committees have been appointed and are now functioning.

At the risk of possibly misjudging some of the criticism of recent months, it might be stated that politics has been a major consideration. The continuing attacks on the State Department and upon United States foreign policy by groups in both Houses of Congress would seem logically to have been reflected in criticism of the Voice of America and other aspects of the information program. Be that as it may, the nature of the criticisms has generally been such that they could scarcely be ignored. The recent 90 per cent cut in the supplemental appropriations for the information program offers sufficient evidence that Congressional criticism is having its effect, in curtailing sykewar funds if in no other way.

But there is another sizable body of criticism which is even more prevalent. This stems from the scholars of psychological warfare—the social scientists, the psychologists, the philosophers—as well as the "professional" propagandists—those with wartime propaganda experience and those in the advertising and public relations fields. These are mostly concerned with the strategy and techniques now being employed. They have no criticism with the program itself, only in the approach to the problem of persuasion.

There are others, of course. Many of the "evaluations" are extremely sound, even though often critical of specific efforts. Unfortunately, most of the "favorable" appraisals of the program have been limited to officials in the State Department.

This chapter includes a variety of such critical evaluations. While somewhat "weighted" in that more critical than favorable examples are included, the weighting was due chiefly to the greater number and variety of critical articles and statements which have appeared in recent months.

REPORT OF THE ADVISORY COMMISSION ON INFORMATION [1]

Our present basic conclusions are these:

That the program is being efficiently administered.

That its personnel has been greatly improved, and is being steadily enriched by specialists of larger experience and talent.

That the expansion authorized by the 81st Congress as the "Campaign of Truth" is being effectively carried forward.

That most of the recommendations made by this Commission have been put into effect.

That a great deal more can be done, and must be done, before the United States will be adequately waging the war of ideas.

That the evaluation techniques through which the Department tests its programs need further strengthening, as much as possible through independent sources.

That grave doubts exist whether major structural changes, such as taking the program outside the State Department, will be an improvement. We are aware of the advantages of a separate agency, but we are more impressed by the disadvantages of divorcing policy-making from operation, and of setting up almost inevitably conflicting representation in foreign countries.

That channels which have been opened up to bring American private expertness into the program in advisory and consultative capacities show great promise of effective results.

[1] From semiannual report to the Congress, United States Advisory Commission on Information. April 1951. p 1-8.

The Commission is most gratified that its recommendations have been largely carried out. The first need, which we began pointing out in 1948, was that career and foreign-service officers in the State Department should become conscious of the vital importance of the information program, and should cooperate effectively with it in Washington and in the field. Much progress has been made in this direction. . . .

Obviously to integrate this new and different kind of foreign operation—the information program—into the long-standing stereotypes of the foreign service is not a job to be accomplished overnight. In some areas in the field, the career men have a deep awareness of the job to be done and a real flair for its techniques. This sort of thing ought to be encouraged at every opportunity. All foreign service officers should be carefully briefed, and repeatedly, on the values of the information program.

As to . . . the program's enlargement, Congress in 1950 went far in its supplemental appropriations to lay the groundwork for an adequate effort. It is immensely gratifying that the real nature of the world crisis was perceived by Congress, and that enough funds to mobilize for ideological warfare were made available. . . . But there is real danger now, in April 1951, that we slip back into complacency.

The situation in Korea to some seems less menacing than it did in mid-1950; the Soviet Union (as we write) has made no new dangerous gestures. Despite grave uncertainties in Iran, Yugoslavia, Indo-China, and elsewhere, American public opinion—manifestly and properly reflected in Congress—is tending to cool off.

We believe, however, that Secretary Marshall was right when he said on March 27 that he regards the present situation as more dangerous than it was six months ago. Therefore we strongly urge that Congress keep right on providing enough ammunition and manpower with which to wage the war of ideas. To cut down the information program at this critical moment would be to court new disasters. Although the tide of Communist influence in Western Europe has been turned back, it is manifest that in vast uncommitted areas of the world, the United States has a long way to go in clarifying its motives and its meaning to peoples. Such clarification requires a major information program. We must not stop or slow up now.

We are particularly gratified at the way in which the information program's personnel has been steadily improved. It takes a great deal of patriotic self-sacrifice for men and women who are highly skilled and highly paid professionals to leave their long-range posts and come into governmental service under conditions of uncertainty and often abuse which have prevailed in recent years. These people deserve the highest recognition and gratitude of their country. There are not a few of them. They have recognized the gravity of the world crisis and they have enlisted voluntarily in the war of ideas. . . .

A year ago the Commission recommended that more attention be given to the evaluation of the impact of the program on the peoples of the world. There was at that time and still is, need for more specific information on how the battle for men's minds is going. Are we hitting the targets toward which the out-flow of information is aimed? How well is the line against the spread of communism being held? Are we winning converts from communism to freedom? It is recognized by the Commission that these are difficult questions, but they are of immense importance for obvious reasons.

The steps taken thus far by the Department towards a more intensive and systematic evaluation of the effectiveness of the program consist of (1) the organization of an Evaluation Staff, at the General Manager's level, composed of six members, concerned primarily with planning and conducting the overall evaluation of the effectiveness of all media in all countries, and (2) the organization of media division evaluation staffs. The largest of these is that of the International Broadcasting Division which now has 74 persons with provision for a total of 102 for 1951. The staffs of the other media divisions are in the process of organization. (3) The allocation of 40 positions to the Research and Intelligence area of the Department for purposes of providing the basic cultural anthropological research for guidance to public affairs officers; maintaining a library of sample foreign propaganda; additional biographical intelligence facilities; analyses and summaries of public opinion surveys; surveys of world reaction to major United States policy moves; analyses of foreign propaganda content; and the collection of intelligence material for the use of USIE. (4) The allocation of USIE field staff positions to the evaluation function on a pilot project basis. Three positions have been allocated to date, one of which is filled at this time.

At present the main activities of the central and special staffs include (1) the screening of reports from USIE field officers for instances of favorable and unfavorable responses, (2) planning studies to be done under contract by private research organizations such as opinion attitude surveys in selected foreign countries; content analyses of media output; media improvement studies; and studies to determine the local communications channels from which the target audiences form their opinions. (A number of such studies have been completed for the International Broadcasting Division).

There are two ways of assessing the effectiveness of any program of public relations, advertising or propaganda. One is to find out if the right things are being said to the right people, in the right ways, and at the right time and through the channels that are most likely to attract attention. It is assumed that if a program comes up to certain standards of quality and quantity it is bound to be effective. The other way is to assess the results by finding out how the program influences the behaviour and beliefs of those to whom it is directed. Thus far the evaluation work of the Department has been mainly of the former type. The Commission notes with satisfaction, however, that plans for 1952 call for studies, in selected areas, of the extent to which people are becoming more favorable toward the cause of freedom as expressed in words and deeds.

The Smith-Mundt Act states that the Commission is expected to report to Congress its independent appraisals, when feasible, of the effectiveness of the program. This has been done in previous reports that have been made at times when one or more members of the Commission have returned from a trip overseas and have had an opportunity for first hand observations.

The Commission has given considerable thought to the question of how it can manage to provide Congress with more comprehensive independent appraisals, within the limits of the time and facilities at its disposal. . . . The Commission has recommended and the State Department has set up seven advisory committees. . . . One of their most useful consequences will be the availability of Committee members for private evaluations of the information program, through their various overseas contacts and trips. On these committees are outstanding national experts in the various media. They will be able to give invaluable help in judging the effectiveness of the program according to the best known standards of communications information.

REPORT OF THE ADVISORY COMMISSION ON EDUCATIONAL EXCHANGE [2]

The expansion of the educational exchange program to many new countries, its rapid increase in volume, and its redirection to meet the challenge of Communist propaganda and subversion, have placed many heavy burdens upon the administrators of the program throughout this three-year period. . . . It is the opinion of the Commission that on the whole the job has been well done. . . .

The Commission wishes to make it clear that we do not believe the program has attained its maturity either in scope or definition. The process of adjusting it to the tasks imposed by the Communist challenge will be a continuous one. To illustrate, we feel that the reexamination of the content of the presentation made to other peoples, as contrasted with the objectives sought, has only just begun. Part of the approach used at one time—the emphasis upon the strength and industrial wealth of the United States for example—ran grave risks of creating

[2] From "Educational Exchange Among Free Nations," fifth semiannual report to Congress of the United States Advisory Commission on Educational Exchange. *Department of State Bulletin*. 24:788-96. May 14, 1951.

envy and resentment, rather than attitudes of cooperation and friendship. We believe that more attention should be given to the development of basic themes for program guidance. Yet it would be very unrealistic to insist that everything must be accomplished at once, and we are unanimous in reporting to the Congress that steady progress has been made over this three-year period in this indispensable but relatively new undertaking. We urge for it increased attention and constructive criticism by the Congress and the public, and further financial support. . . .

Both government and labor have recognized the importance of labor in international relations. The Department of State has labor advisers and consultants, and, at overseas posts, labor attachés and labor reporting officers form a part of the United States diplomatic missions. Under the ECA program and the Department of State's exchange-of-persons program numerous labor representatives have visited the United States. Organized American labor has developed its own technical assistance program which was organized in December 1949 under the sponsorship of the International Confederation of Free Trade Unions (ICFTU), in protest against the Soviet domination of the World Federation of Trade Unions. The ICFTU's program is similar in concept to Point Four activities. Among the many projects initiated by the ICFTU is that of establishing training schools in Asia to prepare promising leaders from countries in the region to function more effectively in the development of free trade unions.

The Commission on Educational Exchange endorses heartily the emphasis being placed on labor by the Department of State. However, we feel that certain additional steps would increase the effectiveness of the Department's activities. Among these are the following which the Commission recommends for consideration by the Department of State: (a) More scholarships at workers' education centers and labor colleges. (b) More planned short-term study tours of trade-unionists on a functional basis. (c) Special summer schools and institutes for labor activists to study social problems and solutions proposed in various countries.

VOA—CHAMPION OF RELIGIOUS FREEDOM [3]

The Voice of America . . . has become the champion of religious freedom in the Iron Curtain countries. Day by day, its broadcasts spark the courage of terrorized Christians who are witnessing the suppression of the outward vestiges of their faith. The Voice is, in addition, one of the few remaining dependable reporters in the Soviet satellite states of religious news there, even going so far as to broadcast complete texts of pastoral letters which many of the clergy dare not read out in the churches. The indignation of Americans and other free peoples over Communist assaults upon the Church is relayed to the scenes of the assaults. And on all important Christian holidays, the Voice of America presents religious services.

The importance that the Voice attaches to the suppression of religious freedom behind the Iron Curtain can be measured by the fact that generally all major developments are broadcast not only to the satellite countries themselves, but in all 28 languages now going out over the frequencies of the Voice. . . .

The cases of Cardinal Mindszenty and Lutheran Bishop Ordass, the arrest of 15 Protestant pastors in Bulgaria, the persecution of Archbishop Beran in Czechoslovakia, and a host of less publicized violations of religious freedom which have scarcely come to the notice of the American public, have constituted a major theme in broadcasts to the Communist sphere. In fact it would be difficult to cite any other one issue into which the Voice of America has put such concentrated effort.

The Voice has had its finger so consistently on the Communist pulse on religious issues that it—the Voice—has known almost as soon as the Communists themselves what is coming next. America's Voice rebuked the arrest of the 15 Protestant pastors in Bulgaria several weeks before the Sofia regime pub-

[3] From "The Iron Curtain Is Not Sound-Proof," by Harriet Rasooli-Sa'eed, free-lance writer. *Presbyterian Life*. 4:8-10. April 14, 1951. Reprinted by permission.

lished the indictment. The ever-tightening noose of suppression upon Archbishop Beran has been exposed, step by step. . . .

So that listeners may know that they are getting not just the reaction of a proportionally infinitesimal group of people working on the VOA, but the sentiments of America en masse—statements by political leaders, patriotic organizations, religious leaders and groups, humanitarians, labor leaders, and the free American press—form the core of Voice of America commentary on the religious issue. . . .

There is scarcely a day when all the broadcasts to the Soviet satellites do not have some item of religious news, with the religious struggle sometimes taking precedence even over the Korean War news. This was the case with Czech broadcasts last November and December, when a group of Czech bishops was on trial on the usual charges of high treason and insubordination; except that this time there was an additional charge of giving texts of pastoral letters to the Voice of America.

Throughout the Soviet-dominated areas of the world, listening to the Voice of America is officially frowned upon but not prohibited by law, because that would be an admission of fear of the Voice. Instead, arrests are made on charges of disseminating false information as reported by the VOA. Sentences are stiff, and sometimes property of the offender is confiscated. This line of attack serves the Communist double purpose of making listening dangerous, and of discrediting information from the Voice. But listening goes on apace.

In Bulgaria there is a well-developed underground for listening. Even small villages usually have two to five shortwave sets capable of picking up VOA broadcasts; and when Communist raiders confiscate the sets, depriving a village of access to the broadcasts, either sets are again supplied by larger towns, or couriers are arranged to carry the texts of the VOA broadcasts daily to the cutoff village. At the outbreak of the Korean War there was not a village in Bulgaria that did not have the news from the Voice of America within twenty-four hours. . . .

In Poland listening is astoundingly widespread. Reports have come from so many different sources that it cannot be doubted that at the hour of VOA broadcasts, streets and cafes in Poland are empty, doctors will not see patients, and lawyers will not receive clients. A Polish DP who is living now in England says that the Voice of America has become a national institution in Poland.

Undercover methods of listening are diverse. Generally groups listen together on one set, but every day a different set. Some leaving home to listen elsewhere will leave a room brightly lighted and Radio Warsaw blaring loudly, with details in the room carefully arranged to give the impression that the occupants have stepped momentarily into another room. In the home where the listening is done the entire house may be darkened and the set even covered with a rug, both to black out its faint glow and to muffle the low murmur of sound. Then listeners must put their heads under the rug to catch the words. Or instead of darkening the rendezvous house, a second set may be placed near a brightly lighted window and tuned loudly to the Communist radio, and stooges planted around it in mock absorption, while the real listening goes on in a darkened back room.

Although the gargantuan struggle between Church and Communist regime goes on in Poland as elsewhere, the Polish clergy have not undergone the brutal treatment given their colleagues in other satellite states. An American citizen recently coming from Poland attributes this to fear of the Voice of America. The Voice has not failed to remind its listeners frequently of the fundamental incompatibility of communism with all religion. . . Further proof that the Voice is drawing blood is the fact that Radio Warsaw has a daily program called *Fala 49* which is devoted solely to refuting VOA broadcasts.

The religious services which the Voice broadcasts on all leading Christian holidays is of deeper significance to Communist-dominated peoples than the ordinary American can understand. Previous to the Communist regime in Bulgaria the Sofia radio broadcast the entire two- or three-hour-long Christmas service from the great cathedral of the capital city. But last Christmas the only religious services on the air in Bulgaria were those from the Voice of America. A Czechoslovakian, writing from Prague of the Easter service in 1949, said, "You gave me hours of choking happiness—a thing hard to find elsewhere today."

The Voice makes a faithful effort to meet the needs of leading religious groupings in each particular country. Christmas messages to Hungary have been given by Msgr. Fulton J. Sheen and the Reverend Samuel Shoemaker of Calvary Episcopal Church in New York City. Last September a special Hungarian Reformation Day service was spot-recorded in the First Hungarian Presbyterian Church in Passaic, New Jersey, for broadcast to Hungary. Gratitude for Voice broadcasts of religious services on the Christian holidays is always indicated by an increased volume of audience mail from nationalities spiritually starved by communism.

EVALUATION OF INFORMATION STRATEGY [4]

We talk of "A Campaign of Truth." This, certainly, is in order. But what is "the truth"? Speeches? Statistics? A day in the life of a Wisconsin farmer? Our congenital dislike of abstract thought has at last come home to roost. *We have failed to determine what it is we wish to communicate.* . . .

And not only have we failed to define *what* we are to say; we have failed to define why we want to say it. Of all the many aims of our propaganda, which is to be primary? Interestingly, almost every private organization that has thought of an overseas propaganda program of its own has stumbled on precisely this question. More to the point, so has the government. . . .

Clearly, something more dynamic is needed. It is too late for mere information. . . . The obstacles to success may seem appalling. For even when we have articulated our philosophy we have the task of projecting it over the tremendous gap in attitudes and environment that separates us from other people. And it is a gap, unfortunately, that we do not readily appreciate.

[4] From "Have We Any Friends?" editorial. *Fortune.* 43:117-20+. February 1951. Reprinted from *Fortune* Magazine by special permission of the editors; copyright 1951 Time Inc.

We have been so unaware of basic differences that we have persisted in talking to the Europeans in terms for which there is no foreign equivalent: *participation, community relations, incentive, public relations, productivity, man-in-the-street, public opinion*—the very listing itself produces a syllabus of the American philosophy. And a glossary of misunderstanding.

Taking the evocative power of these words for granted, we have assumed that "hard facts" will do the job—and that, in a sort of question-and-answer fashion, we can use prepackaged nuggets of truth to beat down each fallacy we come across. It won't work. . . .

But their failure in turn stems from a greater one: our failure to demonstrate the tremendous difference between our capitalism and the capitalism of Europe. . . . To a dangerous degree, our efforts have appeared to the European worker simply a collusion between reactionary blackguards; he still can conceive of American capitalism only in terms of his own—and he is sick of it. It is high time the American businessman realized that it is not European socialism but European capitalism that is the chief block to "free enterprise." "The problem of Europe," as one observer puts it, "comes down to who is to liquidate the capitalists of Europe: the Russians—or the Americans."

Well, there it is. . . . And only recently have we begun doing something about it. After virtually leaving the field to the Russians after the war, in 1948 we authorized the State Department to set up an "information and educational exchange program," and within a year this was further supplemented when ECA's information program was organized. . . . And it wasn't until after Korea that Congress decided a "Campaign of Truth" was in order and voted the money to get it going. . . .

We've fairly new to the game, but—as even the avuncular British concede—we have been learning fast. . . . What have we learned? First, that we need much more of a sharpshooting approach to our "target" groups. There is no "European mind," but scores of group attitudes compounded along all sorts of professional, economic, and geographic lines. And the best way to get at them is through people that talk the separate lingoes.

We have had a hard time talking to European intellectuals, for example, yet so far we have used few intellectuals for the job. . . .

Next, we have learned that one of the principal reasons for the disbelief in American culture is, simply, the high cost of it. Stroll along the Kaertnerstrasse in Vienna, for example, and you will have a hard time finding a bookstore with any decent assortment of moderately priced American books *in German*—that is, until you come to the Communist information center, which has quite an interesting selection. . . . So with the theatre; stiff royalties—payable in dollars—have inhibited widespread production of United States plays. . . . Patently, if we wish to project American culture rather than talk about it, a much more vigorous subsidy program is in order.

More important, we must develop far better means of reaching the masses. Considerable ingenuity has been brought to this problem; our people have put documentary films into thousands of commercial theatres, taken them in trailers to rural villages, brought "showboats" to Mediterranean coastal towns, subsidized troubadours to sing our story in Sicily, floated message-bearing toy balloons all over Europe, distributed household pamphlets and comic books by the millions. But though it is difficult to think of a bet that has been overlooked, we have made only a dent.

Why don't we merely expand all this? The answer, unfortunately, is not that simple. Europe has had a bellyful of propaganda these last ten years, and after a certain point—and it is a very arguable point—you run not only into diminishing returns but rapidly increasing resistance.

There is, however, a way out of the dilemma—the participation of foreign nations in the job. "Let me get the facts about Korea to one pro-United States union man over here," says a United States propagandist, "and he'll be worth a thousand posters." There are many ways to invoke this aid. But there is one so effective, so destructive of the myth, that it has come to be the most promising weapon in our whole armory. . . .

In the summer of 1948, Sir Stafford Cripps and ECA boss Paul Hoffman were talking about productivity. How, Cripps asked, did the Americans do it? . . . "Let's bring your people over," Hoffman answered, "and we'll show them how." So, with great vigor, we proceeded to do. Before long United States firms, labor unions, and professional groups were playing host to scores of European "productivity teams"; by the end of last year over 2,750 had made the trip and returned home—somewhat numbed, but enthusiastic—to tell what they had learned. The result, in increased productivity, is now a well-known story—and a good story it is. But there is another story that is not so well known. What was conceived of as a technical measure turned out to be one of the most effective propaganda tools ever handed us. . . .

Here—in excerpts from productivity-team reports—are some of the things they had to say to their countrymen.

A visit to the United States gives one greater confidence in the ability of democracy to solve its problems. . . . The country is still . . . moving *forward* both culturally, socially, and economically.—(Norwegian trade-unionists)

American unions' attitude to company profits is typical of their acceptance of a capitalist economy. However high, profits, at least in competitive industry, are not regarded as immoral or a social evil; indeed they give proof of solvency and assured employment. . . . The main concern of unions is to obtain a fair share of them.—(British trade-union officials)

Contrary to the impression gained from many American films only a small percentage of American workers and their families live in tenements.—(British trade-union officials)

The big surprise to me was the importance American bosses give to human-relations problems. The American employer seems to be a psychologist aware that his prosperity is tied directly with that of the workers.—(French unionist) . . .

It is difficult for an American to appreciate what revolutionary documents these are. The British trade-union officials' report, for example, became a front-page story and gave British labor a resounding intellectual jolt. The Norwegian report, coupled with the report of a similar team that went to Russia, opened the eyes of left-wingers in a way that all the money in the world would not buy us. Throughout Europe, on a small but appreciable scale, doctrinaires of one kind or another are being provoked to rethink long and dearly held conceptions. . . .

The technical-assistance teams are only one of the ways we have to go about the proselyting job. Thanks to the machinery set up in 1946 and 1948 by the Fulbright and Smith-Mundt acts, and to special programs for Germany, Austria, Finland, China, and Iran, [the Department of] State is bringing over students, teachers, professional people, specialists, and "leaders." The Defense Department is doing the same with Japan. Both State and ECA are placing foreign trainees in United States industry, farms, and government agencies. Altogether, the government is now bringing over about 13,000 people a year for observation, study, teaching, training, and indoctrination. Cost: about $45 million.

But by far the biggest contribution of all has been made by private organizations. This year they will have arranged roughly 40,000 exchanges of their own, and in addition will have footed a large share of the local expenses of many of the people brought over by the State Department. The 4-H clubs have been exchanging young farmers; the Rotary clubs have been bringing over students; the Girl Scouts, "youth leaders"—the list encompasses almost every kind of organization in American community life.

Measured against the need, however, our overall exchange effort has been piddling. (Koreans brought to Moscow between 1946 and 1949: 2,600. Brought to United States in same period: 65.) There is a sort of geometric progression to exchange; since the clue to its success is *applying* the proposition, it follows that the more people engaged in it, the more effective each individual's work becomes.

BASIS OF PSYCHOLOGICAL WARFARE FAILURE [5]

Looked at from the foreign policy point of view, the American psychological warfare program has not been effective. In-

[5] From "Psychological Warfare and Foreign Policy," by Saul K. Padover, Professor of Politics and History in the Graduate Faculty and Dean of the School of Politics in the New School for Social Research; formerly Psychological Warfare Officer, AUS. *American Scholar*. 20, no2:151-61. [April] 1951. Copyright, 1951, by United Chapters of Phi Beta Kappa. Reprinted by permission.

deed, quite the contrary. Two chief misconceptions are largely responsible for the failure. One is the idea that psychological warfare or propaganda is just like advertising. The other is that foreigners think or wish to think like Americans. . . .

It cannot be emphasized too strongly that political propaganda is not the same as selling soap or tissue paper. It is not a job for slick "operators," trained in the art of "putting over a sales campaign." We are not dealing with that kind of campaign. We are dealing with a world revolutionary situation involving races and culture and aspirations totally alien to the experience of advertising executives. . . .

Even in Western Europe, American propaganda fails in its effects when it describes—truthfully, to be sure—the gleaming kitchens, labor-saving devices, and assorted gadgets which the middle-class housewife of the United States has at her disposal. Since the overwhelming majority of European housewives could not possibly afford or ever hope to possess such equipment, the result is either disbelief or resentment. This is particularly true in our propaganda to the Russians, whose standard of living is so low compared to that of the United States that they simply cannot conceive the vastness of the difference. Consequently, statements of American superiority in material things sound to the Russians like sheer lies. The Russians plainly cannot imagine that such things as carpets in every home and cars in workingmen's garages could possibly be true. This is clearly brought out by the comment of Moscow's *New Times*:

> What the Voice of America has to say about workers' housing conditions is no less phony and unconvincing. . . He (the commentator) wants to assure that Americans—all Americans!—live like princes. Here is the rosy picture he paints: "The American worker," he says, "lives either in a separate house or in a separate apartment with kitchen and bathroom. Very many married people prefer to live in the suburbs in a detached cottage with a garden." And he further asserts that the 25 per cent of earnings paid in rent includes gas and telephone and even carpet-cleaning. Carpets, of course, are mentioned here not by chance. The Voice of America wants to insinuate that carpets are as common a thing in America as gas rings.

Even the most truthful statement can boomerang, if it is not geared to the range of the audience's beliefs and expectations.

All reports from Europe and Asia indicate that the United States has failed to win over the masses of people in those parts of the world. This is notably true in Asia, where our policy makers have failed to take into proper account the revolutions that are now convulsing that continent. Leadership of the revolutionary movements there has been virtually abandoned to the Communists. Despite all that, as Reinhold Niebuhr pointed out, "The American nation is grossly overestimating its moral standing in Asia." The truth is, the United States has little prestige left there. Washington's psychological warfare program has hardly made a dent among the masses of . . . undernourished peoples.

It is clear that the best radio transmitters in the world and the most far-flung organization of information specialists are no substitute for policy and leadership. United States policy has been singularly deficient in this moment of world crisis. It has been largely negative: *against* communism, *against* Sovietism, *against* dictatorship. But *for* what? To a world in fear and in need, a humanity in the agony of upheaval, the rich and powerful United States has offered no inspirational ideal or positive social program. As Maury Maverick once said: "You cannot fill the baby's bottle with liberty." Faced with a Communist-led ideological challenge, we have offered no Wilsonian Fourteen-Points program, no Rooseveltian Four-Freedoms appeal. And it is an axiom that you cannot beat something with nothing.

In consequence, our psychological warfare, even as our foreign policy, which it reflects, suffers from intellectual and spiritual emptiness. Perforce it must continue to do so until such a time as the United States shall have formulated a positive program for action, an ideal around which to rally men. Short of that, we are in danger of talking only to those of our friends who already share our expectations, and of losing the great majority of mankind that is still searching for a hope and a vision.

MISTAKEN EMPHASIS ON WORDS: BERNAYS [6]

We are involved in a worldwide clash of ideas. What the United States stands for needs to be made more meaningful to peoples outside our country. . . . The Voice of America is attempting to do this. . . . Almost exclusively the use of words is emphasized in this psychological offensive. We assume that the broadcasting of words about the United States will effect the changes in attitudes we are looking for. . . .

Recent findings of both the social sciences and practical experience show that this overpowering belief in the efficacy of words for such purposes is based on a fallacy. Words, by themselves, cannot do the job. In the process of persuasion, the disposition of the listener to believe or disbelieve the words often is stronger than the power of the words by themselves.

The truth shall make us free, says the Bible. But the power of the truth depends more on our readiness to accept or reject it, than on the truth itself. Recent history has shown that whole nations perceive truth as a lie, and the lie as truth, if they are so disposed.

The many people throughout the world, outside the boundaries of Russia, who believe the Kremlin's lies and promises, show that truth is not necessarily the sole basis for the acceptance or rejection of words. If truth, per se, were the only criterion of acceptance, the Soviets would never have achieved as much acceptance as they have. The Kremlin lied or falsified the deeds of facts, which we would not or could not do.

Researches made by the Information and Education Division of the United States Army indicate that information and skills can be conveyed by words. Opinions or motivations are much less responsive to change through word-propaganda, at times wholly unresponsive. A recent study published by Columbia University's Bureau of Applied Social Research says:

> Persons uninterested or hostile to the persuader's case will deliberately avoid the communicated material; or, if they cannot avoid it, will tend to forget it, or to recast it to fit their already existing attitudes. . . .

[6] From "Winning of the War of Ideas," by Edward L. Bernays, public relations expert. New York *Herald Tribune*. 111:8. February 17, 1951. Reprinted by permission.

Actions speak louder than words. This fact which mankind has known for millennia has now been confirmed by laboratory findings. A realistic approach to the problem of projecting the American point of view effectively through the Voice of America would be to place emphasis on deeds. The problem America faces today is not one of hurling down avalanches of words on the rest of the world, of building the biggest and most copious information service. It is rather a problem of sending out credible words that will be believed because they describe meaningful action.

This, first of all, requires reorientation in planning and carrying out national policy in foreign affairs. Any effective effort to "sell" America to the rest of the world demands that foreign policy and so-called domestic policy both be geared to the impression we want to create in foreign countries. . . .

In addition, the Voice of America is hampered by another major lack—that is, its remoteness from the policy-making decisions of the State Department. . . . Often policy is determined at top levels without regard to the impact it will make on foreign peoples. Or policy may be different from the words that have been disseminated before policy was made.

Action taken by high level State Department policy makers may have an entirely different impact on foreign groups than was intended. These Voice of America men function on a one-way basis, outgoing, rather than on a two-way basis, incoming and outgoing—a prerequisite to sound public relations.

All of this would indicate that until and unless there is a closer relationship between policy making and the words put out over the air, large sums of money are wasted because words and actions don't match up. There is little integration between policy making and articulation.

The Voice of America also wrestles with the problem of an inadequate supply of qualified men to handle the complicated problems of communication over the Voice of America. . . . The Voice of America has an important job to do at this time. The men now grappling with the problem have an understanding of these deeper questions of policy and practice. But until and unless the American public recognizes these broader implications of policy and practice and acts on some of them, the

Voice of America will continue with its principal reliance on words, when in actuality the deeds they stand for expressed in meaningful words are the factors that will bring victory.

THE MUMBLE IN THE VOICE OF AMERICA [7]

Iranians get a half-hour United States program daily, part of it, until recently, by relay from the government-controlled station in Teheran. They get four to six hours a day of Communist party programs broadcast from outside Iran. But the difference in time is less important than the fact that Iranians like the programs from the USSR better than the American ones. The Soviet programs tell them what is going on inside Iran, give news which the government would like to suppress, and never hesitate to criticize any potentially unpopular move on the part of the government itself. The "commercials," Soviet Communist party propaganda, are liberally sandwiched in. . . . It is the "commercials" that do the selling; and when it comes to them, those of the United States do not seem to have much pulling power. Yet in the various suggestions put forth for getting more punch into America's message not one hinted at the possibility that perhaps the real trouble lay in the fact that, although the United States was vigorously saying, "Don't buy from our competitor," it was mumbling when it came to the name and virtues of its own product. . . .

Efforts expended in fighting the social and economic *ideals* of communism are largely wasted. These are something which the people of any nation (if we truly believe in self-determination and democracy) must decide for themselves. Try as it will, the American government, faced with such an obvious risk, cannot bring itself to go whole-hog for democracy as its objective and world ideal.

Uncomfortably spiked on this dilemma, we have been unable to take or to project a propaganda line that can stand up against the sharp single-mindedness of Communist party propaganda.

[7] From an article by William H. Wells, free-lance writer, formerly advertising executive and information officer for the UN. *Harper's Magazine.* 202:23-7. January 1951. Reprinted by permission.

The current Voice of America line under which the United States is countering lies with the truth about American life, is feeble to most of those who hear it. An account of how county government works in the United States, or of how the women of an American town worked to promote child health, is meaningless to people for whom the conditions of life are utterly different, and who want to know how *they* can escape from poverty and misery. The question is: What is the United States offering, in actions, not words, that has a stronger appeal to masses of poverty-ridden people than whatever the Communist party is offering? At present the United States is offering individual freedom, the *status quo* for private property and enterprise, and the right of everyone to have a voice in the government *provided* this does not mean upsetting either private property or private enterprise.

It is this awkward attempt to ride both horses—free democracy and protected capitalism, so natural a team to the people of the United States but so incompatible to the people of many other non-Communist nations—that leads to the mumble in America's foreign propaganda voice. . . . It is the fact that we stand for the right of a people to *choose for themselves* what they shall do and have, rather than to be in the grip of a tyrannical minority which chooses for them, that is our strongest potential asset in the battle of words. We do not take enough advantage of this fact.

For the United States—now engaged in actual war—has been, and still is, unable to make up its mind whether it is fighting for the preservation of capitalism or of democracy. There is no question that our American ideal is democratic capitalism. But it is equally clear that in the United States democratic capitalism has taken an advanced and enlightened form which has few counterparts elsewhere in the world; that in many other nations capitalism and private property rights connote an exploitation of the many by the few which would be shocking to most Americans; and that for these nations capitalism cannot be the ideal (nor in fact the answer). And these are apt to be the very nations by whose side, or even on whose territory, the United States may have to fight. . . .

In view of this hard, if unpalatable, fact, the United States is being forced to an extremely difficult decision: to support democracy, regardless of the outcome, or to support capitalism even if it means letting democracy go by the boards. . . .

The principle of supporting democracy (which in practice means government by the majority with equal rights for all) is made all the harder to embrace because it can lead in so many different directions: to the New Deal as in the United States; to socialism as in Britain; even to the tyranny of Nazism as in Germany. Here democracy's own inner paradox becomes apparent: on the one hand faith in the majority of the people to be right, on the other the realization that the majority might turn out to be wrong.

CRITIQUE OF VOICE PROGRAMMING [8]

What does the Voice say? The answer is that it both talks and sings. . . . It has three types of programs—music, news and analyses, and features. . . . The music . . . is a matter of taste that cannot be easily evaluated. The features are likely to be regarded as amiable propaganda. They are not infrequently characterized by a bland assumption that what interests Americans is necessarily of interest to foreigners. The rather flat and obvious typescript samples this writer has read violated the first rule of good propaganda—Know thy audience. . . .

As for the Voice of America's news program, that is of considerable potential importance, primarily if and as it reaches people behind the Iron Curtain. Here again the Voice of America is not sufficiently psychological in its approach to the news. News is not an objective quality like mathematics but one that necessarily depends on the hearers' background, general information and expectations. Still, the Voice of America's reporting of certain events, for example the trial of Cardinal Mindszenty, forces the totalitarian governments to publish news which they would otherwise prefer to suppress. In general, however,

[8] From "Psychological Warfare," by Saul K. Padover, Dean of the School of Politics, New School for Social Research. Foreign Policy Association, *Headline Series No. 86*. March-April 1951. p23-56. Reprinted by permission.

this is a field that still has to be worked over imaginatively by the combined insights and imaginations of journalists, social scientists, historians and others.

CRITICISM OF VOICE NEWS AND COMMENTARY [9]

The average Voice news analysis program is as lack-lustre as a State Department directive. The Voice's typical commentary shows are painfully dull, pompous, didactic and laden with enough diplomatic clichés to put even the most avid White Paper enthusiast to sleep. . . .

Measured by simple universal prose standards . . . the typical Voice analysis program lacks imagination, appeal, clarity and common sense. Judging from a number of random scripts, the recipe appears to be: Use plenty of big-sounding soporifics, like "the monolithic structure of communism," even if you don't know what they mean (swell for impressing the boss with your erudition); mix well with plenty of quotes from the New York *Times* editorials, giving credit for same (convenient for filling up time); water down freely with phrases like "allegedly," "it is reliably reported" and "nevertheless," except where you want to ridicule communism; throw the book at the Communists without exercising subtlety, appeal or imagination even if you happen to sound offensive to potential listeners in and out of the free nations (don't worry; thumbnosing the Commies looks good on your job record).

If International Broadcasting Division, which operates the Voice, has any real talent on its whopping payroll, the programs don't show it. Many a Voice script reads like a likely candidate for *New Yorker* magazine's "infatuation with sound of own words department." Here are some samples from a five-page script delivered earlier this year under the title, *Soviet Russia, Shadow and Substance*:

"The Soviet regime continues to box at shadows and to avoid substance" (Page 2).

[9] From "Washington, Paris Agree: Propaganda Lays an Egg," by Ben Atlas, Washington correspondent of *The Billboard*. *The Billboard*. 63:3. March 3, 1951. Reprinted by permission.

"Everywhere we see the Soviet regime hitting vigorously at shadows. . . ." (Page 3). . . .

"Why this constant boxing at shadows?" (Page 5).

"It may well be that the Soviet leaders will continue to box at shadows. . ." (Page 5).

As though paucity of ideas were not enough to deaden the script, the Voice rarely resists using polysyllabic mouth-fillers where simple English could do the trick. Here, for instance, is one of the ways the Voice answered that question, "Why this boxing at shadows?" "The answer," intoned the Voice, "lies in what Foreign Minister Kardelj of Yugoslavia has called the 'hegemonistic tendencies' of the Soviet State." . . .

[One] commentator wrestled himself into a verbal head-lock in what started out to be a refutation of some rantings of Soviet propagandist Peter Pospelov. First the Voice commentator quoted at length from Pospelov's utterances, thus using America's powerful overseas transmitters to give further circulation to Pospelov's propaganda. Declared the Voice commentator:

> The United States, he (Pospelov) asserted, was the arch-enemy of the Soviet regime and the Russian people. It had worked to destroy the Soviet Union ever since the October revolution. "The blood of the Russian people," said Pospelov, "stains the hands of the American imperialists."

The Voice pundit then declared:

> This sentence which served as the keynote for Pospelov's long tirade of hate is remarkable for two reasons: First, because of the magnitude of the lies that it uttered; second, because in a physical sense Pospelov was dangerously close to the genuine truth at the very moment he was voicing his big lie.

The Voice commentator spent several minutes trying to untangle himself from that last one. Unfortunately, he never did succeed. His recitation had about as much impact as a reading of a city telephone directory. Typical:

> But it is hard to believe that this campaign can achieve its purpose. For, as a recent State Department declaration dealing with Pospelov's speech points out, the Russian people themselves must sense the untruth of Pospelov's statements. . . .

A program that ought to be one of the liveliest in the Voice repertoire is the five-day-a-week "report from Washington." This one, in three successive days heard by this writer last week, reached depths of boredom. The program starts with news headlines from New York City. It shifts to the nation's capital for "on-the-spot" news and commentaries, and then returns to New York for last-minute news. The headlines are much too sparse to be informative, and the commentaries tedious.

On one afternoon last week the commentator reported to his audience that Capitol Hill was relatively quiet, and he went on to relate that there was a congressional hearing that day on defense production, told who some of the witnesses were, but failed to mention a word of what was said at the hearing.

Reporting non-committally on some other events, he used time-consuming phrases like, "the President emphasized the need for quick action, and it is believed that this quick action will be forthcoming." . . .

A sidelight on some of the Voice thinking was provided by one International Broadcasting Division spokesman . . . who, when told of the Washington show's tediousness, said the program aimed for a target of "high-level people, like British journalists and statesmen. What's important is that it comes from Washington; that means it's authentic," he said with solemnity which made it impossible for him to have his tongue in his cheek.

CRITICISM OF NEWS HANDLING: TABER OF NEW YORK [10]

I recognize, as we all do, the absolute necessity in these days of a real Voice of America—patriotic, competent and able to present America's picture to the world. I should support it if it cost $200 million instead of a $100 million if we had that kind of a Voice. Today we have no voice whatever on the air. . . .

I talked with Mr. Barrett first on the 29th of June—four days after the Russian-inspired break in Southern Korea. . . .

[10] From remarks on the floor of the House of Representatives by Congressman John Taber of New York. *Congressional Record*. 96:13726-7. August 26, 1950.

I asked him for the broadcasts for the 26th, 27th and 28th of June. . . . There was not, in any of the broadcasts, the slightest word that could be considered as propaganda in behalf of the United States position, nor did any of these broadcasts name Russia as the aggressor. All that the broadcasts consisted of was newscasts, and these very poorly done.

Was that because of a policy of the State Department not to tell the world where the United States stood, or was it because of the total lack of competence and loyalty on the part of the United States Information Service? Mr. Barrett himself, at that time, had not made a business of reading the broadcasts. . . .

On the 19th of July . . . I asked him for the broadcasts for the 18th of July. I received them in due course and examined them. At that time there had been no improvement whatever; not a word was said against Russia; they kept talking about Communists but never named Russia as the aggressor—responsible for the mess that they had created in the world.

This time the newscasts were just as poorly done as before but there was more. There was the story of the Tydings committee and its report; Mr. Tydings' comments against Senator McCarthy and Senator McCarthy's reply. Both indicating that there was a very large segment of our population that did not believe in the loyalty of its own State Department.

How such a thing could be broadcast by the Voice of America—advertising the situation that careless administration has brought about—is beyond me. They all referred to labor troubles in the United States which would be most handy for Russia to exploit. They gave a lot of play to the fact that the Republicans and the Democrats were fighting over foreign policy.

I again called Mr. Barrett on the 15th of August and asked for the broadcasts for the 14th of August. I received the broadcasts and have examined them.

There is one improvement. They have broadcast the voice of Warren Austin, the United States Delegate to the United Nations, and he named Russia as the aggressor. But that was not followed up in a single instance with anything affirmative on the part of any of the broadcasters operating for the so-called Information Service, and by waiting so long in naming Russia as the aggressor we lost the initiative in the propaganda war.

We are not presently making use of our facilities and we are using a shortwave 100,000-watt station at Frankfurt to broadcast to the troops when regular band broadcasts would get to them just as well and this station could be used for long distance broadcasting.

We have, as I understand it, a 40,000-watt station that is not set up at all. We have many stations around the territory near the Iron Curtain that could broadcast, on regular bands, items that would get through to the Iron Curtain countries. Not one radio in ten in the United States is equipped for shortwave, and I would not expect any better percentage in any of the countries behind the Iron Curtain.

Frankly, I demand that the so-called Voice of America become the Voice of America; become militant; become a fighting force designed to get the true picture of the United States across to the world. I do not expect to offer a motion to strike out the funds for this item although that would be the proper way to get efficiency—to force them to reform before they were given more money.

THE GREEN-FERGUSON REPORT TO THE SENATE [11]

Calling for "complete reorientation" of State Department's Voice of America, Senator Theodore F. Green (D., R. I.) and Senator Homer Ferguson (R., Mich.), in a formal report to the Senate on a recent global mission, declared they "found ample evidence that our Voice of America, our State Department, and our American foreign policy have not been successful in meeting the Communist propaganda."

Based on a congressionally authorized first-hand survey of conditions abroad, the report contrasts sharply with the State Department's self-laudatory evaluations of Voice results. Capitol Hill is attaching high significance to the Green-Ferguson report not only because of the high caliber of the authors and the criti-

[11] From "Senators Ferguson and Green Ask 'Voice' Reorientation," by Ben Atlas, Washington correspondent of *The Billboard*. *The Billboard*. 63:1+. May 5, 1951. Reprinted by permission.

cal view they have expressed, but also because theirs is the first official evaluation of the Voice by an outside group without formal State Department ties. Previous official appraisals had their origin in the State Department itself or in advisory bodies directly attached to the State Department.

The Green-Ferguson report suggested the feasibility of decentralizing the Voice program so as to channel United States propaganda "through native minds and native tongues" overseas. The report indicated a lack of reality in the current Voice approach. The Senate pair's findings were reached after talks with more than 200 officials in 16 countries in several parts of the globe during a month's tour last December in representing Congress at the Commonwealth Parliamentary Association meeting in Canberra, Australia, on "foreign relations defense."

With Voice operations under mounting criticism, several proposals have been made on Capitol Hill for a sweeping examination. An impartial analysis of Voice programming recently showed programs overburdened with diplomatic gobbledygook, naive moralizing, unintelligent defensiveness, unreality, and a general tone of bureaucratic piety.

Senators Green and Ferguson in summarizing their report declared:

Almost everywhere we found unrest with violence flaring up from time to time over a variety of issues. We found countries so paralyzed by fear of another world war that they are willing to surrender almost everything to the Communists for peace, ignoring the fact that peace cannot be achieved by surrender.

We found narrow self-interest, which amounted to isolationism in its pure form. Nations appeared willing to deal with communism only in terms of their own interests. The larger view of a free world cooperative defense against aggression was remote. That is why we have received so little real support for our action in Korea.

We found simple, unrealistic, and almost childlike ignorance of the Communist danger, with nerve centers deadened to the meaning of communism through overexposure to the doctrines of socialism and the all-powerful state.

Everywhere in the Far East and in the Near East we saw evidences of shrewd, insidious Communist propaganda. It was handled by natives who were won over and educated in Moscow to communism. It exploited every complaint, every hope, every fear, and every condition in each country in order to induce the people to hate America and the West, and to embrace communism.

> We found ample evidence that our Voice of America, our State Department, and American foreign policy have not been successful in meeting the Communist propaganda.
>
> Our failures in the area of psychological warfare [stated the report] are to be contrasted with undeniable Communist successes.
>
> We can learn much from the basic Communist technique, which transmits its propaganda through native minds and native tongues. A basic recommendation is complete reorientation of the United States information service, and particularly the Voice of America. Without decreasing the effective scope of the information program, it is suggested that no less than the funds now expended for the program be directed to a decentralized program, which will function primarily through or in conjunction with the diplomatic missions within the various countries involved. This is designed to achieve maximum efficiency by pin-pointing objectives.
>
> As firmly and as candidly as possible, members of the delegation attempted at every formal and informal conference to state the attitude of the American people toward world issues—as we understand that attitude. We felt that our (Senator Green's and Ferguson's) plain speaking was appreciated at all times. We believe that our international position has suffered from a lack of candor and plain speaking on the part of some emissaries and policy makers. Differences inevitably occur among peoples. But, in the present atmosphere of tension and uncertainty throughout the world, these differences are best resolved on a basis of candor and plain speaking.

Representative Cliff Clevenger (R., O.), commenting on the report, went even further to declare that the Voice lacks "a real directing head" and that United States representatives in the capitals abroad are finding "much of this stuff" put out by the Voice "is literally poison in the country which it reaches." Clevenger asserted, "We will find, as we found in Iran, that we could not maintain over 30 minutes of propaganda in 24 hours without more pressure from her neighbors than she could withstand." Clevenger said the Voice's "pattern of material" has been furnishing "a more perfect background for Russian attack on us than you could possibly conceive."

On this score, Senator Green describing conditions in Belgium, stressed in the report the necessity of having "an adequate answer to Soviet propagandists who talk constantly about the dangers of Western imperialism, about consequences of German rearmament, and about that awful country, the United States, with its low culture, race discrimination, and gangsterdom."

Green continued as follows:

In high authoritative quarters, particular concern was expressed lest our information program might be giving aid and comfort to the enemy by showing too much of the bad or seamy side of American life.

The senator then quoted "one high United States official in Brussels" as declaring:

We seem to feel that we must give the whole picture, all the good and all the bad. Very sensational news material comes abroad which oftentimes paints the United States in a very bad light, whereas Soviet policy is to play up, and not to play down, the Soviet way of life. Can we afford to be so objective at this critical moment? Can't we at least emphasize more of the positive side, since all the world is not so open minded in its appraisal of news as, say, the average American at home?

Senator Green then stated:

Members of the delegation felt this point was extremely well taken and in line with current United States information needs abroad.

Following conferences with heads of states and leaders of government in 16 countries and dependencies, members of the delegation are strongly of the opinion that we have been losing the cold war battles up to now, and that we should speedily do something about it. Indeed, it is imperative that we do so.

MISMANAGEMENT OF VOICE: ROONEY SUBCOMMITTEE [12]

The House Appropriations Committee gave blanket approval to the report of its subcommittee, headed by Representative John J. Rooney (D., N.Y.), which not only slashed the $97.5 million supplemental Voice outlay to $9,533,939, but also lopped off $1.5 million from another outlay which the Voice had intended to splurge for a building in New York City.

The Rooney subcommittee report, climaxing months of painstaking examination of Voice operations, contained the most

[12] From "House Report Says 'Voice' Is Mismanaged," news story. *Variety*. 82:1+. April 11, 1951. Reprinted by permission.

blistering criticism of the Voice ever placed on record by any congressional group. The subcommittee emphasized that it has supported the Voice idea since its inception and that a "great need" exists for "combatting insidious propaganda emanating from the Kremlin." The report continued:

> However, the committee must say that it is very much disappointed in the accomplishments and progress made to date (by the Voice of America). Mismanagement and poor planning with regard both to the engineering and to the administrative phases of the program have cost valuable time as well as dollars.

The subcommittee's report, and the full committee's adoption of it, will have the effect of putting the State Department's Voice of America on probation before it can get the remainder of the $97.5 million outlay which Congress had earmarked to be spent over a three-year period for construction of transmitters.

President Truman earlier this year sent Congress a special message asking for the whole outlay immediately. The Truman message came after criticism of Voice mismanagement had begun mounting on Capitol Hill. State Department, which has been staging a well-heeled propaganda drive to fatten its Voice purse, is figured as having master-minded the Truman request in order to get as much money committed to the Voice as possible before any full-dress examination of the program got under way on Capitol Hill. Three separate resolutions for Voice inquiries are pending in the Senate.

It is known that congressmen examining the Voice have been shocked by evidences of waste and mismanagement such as fat expenses for globe-trotting junkets and heavy outlays for inept personnel responsible for sour programming. . . .

The Rooney subcommittee report pointed out that State will be able to complete seven transmission projects through $45 million already allocated, and the $9.5 million which the subcommittee allowed out of the supplemental budget. State wanted to rush 13 other projects.

> Testimony before the committee [said the report] indicated that lack of proper planning, poor management, and avoidable delays in the execution of plans and contracts have been considerable factors occa-

sioning the necessity of the request for over $9.5 million additional for the above projects for which $44,687,184 in appropriations have already been made.

The subcommittee said that testimony also indicated that

All of the sites for the requested 13 new and additional facilities for which $88,966,061 was requested, have not as yet been selected.

In fact, the committee was informed that no definite determinations have yet been made as to the countries for which some of these proposed facilities would be located [continued the report]. It was further testified that a number of these proposed facilities might be located on ships, although, on questioning, the committee was given only vague and incomplete estimates of the number and the costs of such facilities as compared with land installations. Field tests of the transmitters proposed for the planned facilities have not as yet been made. Such tests are now scheduled to be made this month. The material submitted to the committee in support of the estimate lacked definiteness and was so devoid of specific data that it could not be considered a plan of action.

The so-called Voice of America has received the support of this committee since its inception. The committee fully believes in a strong, effective Voice of America. It feels that there is a great need for combatting the insidious propaganda emanating from the Kremlin by making the truth available to those behind the Iron Curtain and to mankind the world over. It wholeheartedly believes that, properly managed and directed, the Voice of America is the best medium for accomplishment of a campaign of truth that has yet been conceived. However, the committee must say that it is very much disappointed in the accomplishments and progress made to date. Mismanagement and poor planning with regard both to the engineering and to the administrative phase of the program have cost valuable time as well as dollars.

FURTHER EVIDENCE—ROONEY [13]

Representative John J. Rooney (D., N. Y.) said Congress supplied funds last year to the Voice to purchase 200,000 small radio sets at $15 each for distribution inside the Iron Curtain. However, he asserted, none of the sets has been distributed, although they have been bought, in England, for $35 each.

[13] From "90% Slash for 'Voice' Budget Gets House OK," news story. *Variety*. 82:29+. April 11, 1951. Reprinted by permission.

THE LOSING BATTLE IN INDIA [14]

Very few of India's 400,000 radio sets—one for every [800] persons—are ever tuned in on the Voice of America. It is not because listeners don't want to hear the American broadcasts. The fact is quite to the contrary. Indians are anxious to hear both sides, but so far as radio propaganda is concerned, the Soviet Union and its satellites have a virtual monopoly on the Indian air waves.

This situation exists simply because the Voice of America has no transmitter near enough or with a sufficiently powerful beam to be heard at favorable hours, whereas the powerful Russian stations can be received with moderately priced sets virtually around the clock. The Voice of America is heard best in India late at night when few persons are listening in this early-rising country.

Also, the Voice of America's wave length is so close to that of All-India Radio, the Soviet stations and the big transmitter in Ceylon, that it suffers constant interference aside from Soviet jamming.

So we are letting the radio war go by default. If it is not possible to build a transmitter sufficiently close, or to penetrate the wall of interference, the next best proposition is to purchase time on Radio Ceylon, which is heard clearly in this whole area. [Agreement announced April 1951.]. . .

The friendliness of Indian newspapers needs to be cultivated by personal contact with editors. Without more of this, most of the voluminous press material supplied by the USIS meets the usual fate of handouts that are heaped on every editor's desk. They go into the wastebasket.

The USIS is now mailing American news bulletins to many media, and it is hoped to improve this service when a new budget permits expansion of the staff. Lack of personnel, which means

[14] From "Battle of Propaganda: Reports from Two Posts in Asia—Native Communists, Spreading Ideas that Reach Them from Moscow, Hold a Great Advantage over the United States—Soviet Has India's Ear," by Robert Trumbull, New York *Times*. 99:E5. August 20, 1950. Reprinted by permission. (Also reprinted in *Congressional Record*. 96:13086-7. August 21, 1950.)

lack of money, prevents the USIS from doing many things that might be done to win the propaganda war.

Recently the USIS distributed 20,000 copies of the American white paper on Korea and saw that one was handed to every member of Parliament before the Indian legislative body held its debate on Korea.

USIS libraries in the major cities are popular, but American literature is scarce on the bookstalls while Soviet books and pamphlets are plentiful everywhere. The Communists charge for all their reading matter, although only a few cents. This seems to make it more valuable than the free American material. Conversely, commercially published American literature is far too expensive for the average Indian.

An effective means of putting across the American point of view is now being exploited here—the exchange program financed under the Fulbright and Smith-Mundt acts. Indian editors, scholars and others sent to the United States under the various categories of this program usually return here impressed and friendly. Journalists and speakers who have personally experienced the American way of life are often powerful vehicles—of their own accord—for spreading our point of view.

We suffer another disability in this propaganda war that the Russians do not. Indians do not like to feel that they are being propagandized. Therefore, American operations in this field are suspect and sometimes have an effect opposite to the one intended. But somehow the Russians get away with it. Probably that is due partly to innate leftist tendencies in the Asians. Closely related to this is an underprivileged people's resentment of American prosperity. Our demonstration of the benefits of free enterprise must be handled with extreme tact.

What is needed to deal more effectively with the Communist propaganda legions here [in India] is to make America's story available to more people through radio and inexpensive literature, which should be made plentiful everywhere in the local languages

AFRS TOPS PROPAGANDA VOICE IN EUROPE [15]

If overseas mail, reports from foreign countries and servicemen's views are any criteria, then Armed Forces Radio Service, with its comparatively meager operating budget of $1.5 million, is doing a far better job of public relations than Voice of America. . . . In arguing the point, it is brought out that AFRS, working out of the Armed Forces Information and Education Division, Office of Secretary of Defense, is beamed directly at the GI overseas, while Voice, guided by the State Department, specializes in propaganda, seeking, and in most cases succeeding, to penetrate the Iron Curtain countries. Facts brought to light this week show that AFRS, with its listening audience of 90 million, is actually reaching the areas Voice does and is achieving the results sought by Voice bigwigs.

An estimated 88 million foreign civilians are known to eavesdrop on AFRS broadcasts. While AFRS programming is such as to inform and educate the American GI away from home, it is found enjoyable to citizens who completely ignore Voice programs. Hundreds of letters arrive weekly at the AFRS office here, telling personnel how "wonderful it is that America thinks enough of its fighting men to give them shows, music, news and sports highlights." This sentiment is borne out by visitors to other countries who, while AFRS broadcasts are not . . . [scheduled] in newspapers, have no trouble locating the AFRS shows due to the popularity of these shortwave and platter . . . [segments] with European and Asiatic citizenry.

AFRS is reaching into Iron Curtain satellites as is witnessed by jamming and garbling of newscasts. Music, strangely enough, is accepted by Stalin and his aides which only accentuates that old chestnut about music being the international language.

How AFRS manages to retain its foreign interest with a budget many times less than Voice, is not known. AFRS maintains 54 overseas stations. . . . AFRS outlets in Munich and outside Tokyo are 200,000-watters, largest in the world. With

[15] From "Good Will Builder: AFRS Tops 'Voice's' Public Relations Job," news story. *The Billboard*. 63:8. May 12, 1951. Reprinted by permission.

adequate shortwave facilities, AFRS 200,000-watt transmitters can beam to any place in the world.

Just where Voice seems to have failed as far as establishing a link between this country and other nations, has been rehashed many times. Whether it's poor management, too much extravagance, improper approach to foreign thinking or structurally weak material content, cannot be honestly decided at this time. It remains paradoxical that an [organization] . . . with a $1.5 million allocation should outdraw Voice with its large-scale planning and over 3,000 staff of writers. But when results are tallied, then AFRS is far ahead of present Voice of America programming.

PROPOSALS FOR MORE EFFECTIVE TACTICS

EDITOR'S INTRODUCTION

Criticism of the American psychological warfare program has perhaps one outstanding attribute—it has stimulated public discussion and interest more than would otherwise be possible. The result has been scores of suggestions and recommendations from people in every walk of life. Most of these proposals have dealt with the Voice of America, which is the chief weapon in the propaganda arsenal, and has caught the public fancy as well.

Ideas for improving the sykewar program range all the way from tying leaflets to balloons and letting them blow over Soviet territory to building a television network in all the free nations of the world, particularly in the areas of greatest illiteracy. At the top level is the creation of a new Psychological Warfare Board to establish overall propaganda policy for all branches of the government in international relations, including the activities of the Defense Department. At the other extreme, perhaps, is the "tub-thumping" drive for all-out subversive propaganda against the Soviet Union and the satellite countries. This latter group would leave the information program in the Department of State as an "official" organ dealing primarily with news, in most instances. The real sykewar offensive would be in private hands—privately operated radio stations, establishing and encouraging underground and revolutionary movements behind the Iron Curtain, sabotage and other subversive activities.

In between are the recommendations for tactical improvement—asking for redefinition of aims, suggesting concrete lines of attack to reach certain groups, Benton's "Marshall Plan of Ideas" among others.

The proposals included here are by no means a complete list. Many of these recommendations have been worked out carefully in detail, but because of limitations of space were necessarily condensed to bare outlines. Their major significance lies in the fact that psychological warfare, as yet, has no rules. No idea or plan can be ignored, no matter how preposterous it might sound. And it might well be some utterly fantastic scheme that could provide the victory in the war for the minds and loyalties of men.

In the immediate future there appears to be no hope of a return to normalcy. Overseas propaganda is a permanent program of national policy in the United States. The information program is a major instrument of foreign policy, supplementing and to a large extent supplanting the traditional diplomatic function. Whether the cold war grows colder or develops into a hot war, psychological warfare has become well established as a governmental operation and there is every indication that it will continue to be highly important for many years to come. Even now, the information and educational exchange operations of the United States are half of the total State Department operations—both in size of staff and in budget. If current plans are carried out, this disproportion between information and foreign policy will increase even more in the next year or two.

Therefore, it seems highly important to consider every aspect of the present program, its effectiveness, and how it might be made more effective in increasing mutual understanding between the United States and other nations, as well as telling America's story abroad.

RECENT DEVELOPMENTS IN AMERICA'S PSYCHOLOGICAL WARFARE PLANS [1]

Mounting evidence of unrest among peoples behind the Iron Curtain has reinforced demands that the United States, without relaxing the drive to build up military defenses, launch a vigorous nonmilitary offensive to undermine Communist influence and rally the forces of freedom. An indication that the administration may be preparing a move in that direction has been given by reports that President Truman is studying plans for full integration of cold-war activities. Formation of a body in the nature of a political general staff, to take over top direction of United States policy in a stepped-up nonmilitary offensive against communism is . . . under consideration. (General Eisenhower, testifying last July 5 before a Senate Foreign Relations subcommittee, proposed creation of "a general staff of a new kind," composed of eminent men serving without pay on a rotating basis, to direct the activities of an agency handling every phase of propaganda in a great truth offensive.)

An interdepartmental National Psychological Strategy Board, under the chairmanship of the Assistant Secretary of State for Public Affairs, was set up in mid-August 1950 to coordinate "foreign information and psychological strategy in situations

[1] From "Non-Military Weapons in Cold-War Offensive," by Buel W. Patch, senior member of research staff, *Editorial Research Reports.* 1:259-67. April 12, 1951. Reprinted by permission.

where joint action by more than one agency of the government is required in this field." . . . A conflict of views between the State Department . . . and the Defense Department . . . has [resulted in] . . . a compromise solution, . . . the appointment of a new Psychological Strategy Board responsible jointly to the State and Defense Departments, the Central Intelligence Agency, and the National Security Council, and with a full-time director working under the senior staff of the National Security Council. [This change was effected in June 1951.]. . .

Although the Voice of America has steadily expanded its "campaign of truth" since the international crisis began to deepen, numerous persons have been insisting that the United States should adopt a more aggressive policy in the nonmilitary struggle with the Kremlin. In a panel discussion at Princeton, February 22, for example, Charles D. Jackson, president of the National Committee for a Free Europe, declared that in psychological warfare truth was not enough; what was needed was money and an attitude of "no holds barred and no questions asked." . . .

Harold Stassen, testifying February 23 before the Senate Foreign Relations and Armed Services committees, said measures of military defense should be supplemented by encouragement and assistance for the "many millions of peoples within the Communist prison of nations" who desire liberation from ruthless oppression. On the radio, January 15, Stassen had advocated a "counter-revolution program," organized and executed through an independent agency outside the State Department, to help such peoples resist and overthrow existing regimes. He asserted that the Soviet Union and its satellites were beset with internal discontent and unrest and so were peculiarly vulnerable to counter-revolution.

General William J. Donovan, who headed the wartime Office of Strategic Services, spoke in similar vein in a radio address on March 18. Declaring that the way to preven outright war was to "put aside our own fears and create fear in the mind of the enemy," he called on the country to seize the initiative in the cold war. Americans, Donovan said, were accustomed to think of war in terms of conventional weapons and forces and to prepare accordingly, but he pointed out that since 1945 the

Soviet Union had been waging against this country an unconventional "war of maneuvers by subversive means short of involvement in open hostilities." In the circumstances, he concluded, "We must integrate our own unorthodox resources as we have unified our conventional (armed) services." . . .

George F. Kennan, Russian expert on leave from the State Department, observed recently that . . . "we in the outside world who believe in the cause of freedom will never prevail in any struggle against the destructive workings of Soviet power unless the Russian people are our willing allies."

Refugees from Eastern Europe have applauded, as heartening to their people, the introduction in Congress of bills to establish in the Army of the United States a Volunteer Freedom Corps composed of aliens enlisting for service outside this country. It has been asserted that such a corps would prove a great attraction to young men in exile from their native countries, would stir the hopes of captive peoples for liberation, and might form the nucleus of national units which in event of war would be fed by mass desertions from satellite armies. No action has been taken on the Freedom Corps bills, but the pending draft and universal military training bill . . . contained a provision sponsored by Senator Lodge (R., Mass.) to increase to 25,000 annually for five years the number of aliens who can be recruited by the Army and "integrated into established units."

MARSHALL PLAN OF IDEAS [2]

By far the most imaginative step we have taken in our foreign relations since 1945 has been the Marshall Plan. . . . With this success before us, is it not time—and past time—for us to create a worldwide Marshall Plan in the field of ideas? Let us now aim to close the mental gap between ourselves and the people of the world. . . .

[2] From "The Struggle for the Minds and Loyalties of Mankind—Proposing a Marshall Plan of Ideas," a speech by Senator William Benton from Connecticut before the Senate, March 22, 1950. *Congressional Record*. 96:3821-6. March 22, 1950.

I . . . propose that the United States now undertake to organize its campaign for men's minds and loyalties on a scale commensurate with the need and commensurate with the stakes. . . . Specifically, I propose six steps:

First. Maintenance, through the United Nations and through our own diplomacy, of a steady and steadily increasing pressure in behalf of worldwide freedom of information. . . .

Second. Acceleration of the work of the United Nations Educational, Scientific, and Cultural Organization to the point where, with effective leadership, it has a chance to make a significant, perhaps decisive, contribution to peace.

Third. Development of the activities of the Offices of International Information and Educational Exchange in the Department of State, in the following ways, among many others: (a) Preparation and execution of a comprehensive worldwide program to exhibit documentary and educational motion pictures designed to explain the democratic principles and ideals which underlie our foreign policy. (b) Significant and immediate expansion of our program for bringing foreign students to the United States. (c) Creation of a world broadcasting network capable of broadcasting on long wave, short wave, or medium wave, with an ultimate goal of reaching virtually every radio set in the world. I may say parenthetically, while our present domestic radio and the publicity it gets in the American press is effective, our international radio does not reach an appreciable number of the world's sets with a satisfactory signal. It is a very weak reed. It is indeed, . . . a whisper, not a voice. (d) The use of any and all possible means to reach people who are shut off from the free world by censorship and by suppression.

Fourth. Promotion of democratic education abroad, notably in the occupied areas of Germany and Japan.

Fifth. Convening of a conference of non-Communist nations now conducting international information programs, with a view to reaching a better understanding on common themes and greatly increasing the effectiveness of the projection of such themes.

Sixth. Encouragement of the establishment of a nongovernmental agency to help inspire and guide the efforts of the millions of private American citizens who might use their talents and resources and contacts overseas in futherance of the programs and objectives of this resolution. . . .

We do not feel these six steps cover the field by any means, but we feel that they illustrate how the international propagation of the democratic creed can and should be made an instrument of supreme national policy. . . .

Nothing equals the motion picture in its capacity for gripping and holding masses of people, and communicating information and attitudes in vivid, remarkable form.

If we are in earnest about reaching the minds and touching the loyalties of mankind we must be prepared to carry out a program which would enable us to exhibit documentary motion pictures to at least one fourth of the population of the earth once a month. We need to get the pictures. We do not have them now. . . .

Broadcasting also is a unique medium. It is instantaneous. It is cheap. It can overlap censorship at boundaries. . . .

Unlike publications or motion pictures it can reach remote and rural areas as easily as metropolitan centers. It presupposes no requirement of literacy. It is not affected by shortage of paper or film stock.

But shortwave broadcasting is not enough, even if we had adequate transmitters which we have not. What is required is a unified, worldwide network capable of laying a signal into every receiver in the world—medium wave or long wave as well as short wave. This can be done, despite many obstacles, if we have the will to do it. . . .

Ex-students from America have always been among our best friends abroad. Many of them go home to become leaders of their countries. They do not want to be like us; we do not want them to be; we just want them to know at first hand what is true and untrue about us, and why we are as we are. This they learn when they are here with us, and they are by far our most valuable ambassadors when they return to their homes.

I personally favor an exchange program which would absorb as many as 100,000 foreign students a year, a three or four hundred per cent increase over our present foreign enrollment.

Although there would be much private support, such an extensive program might cost us as much as $100 million a year. That would be two thirds the cost, say, of a new dreadnaught or a battleship or an airplane carrier. . . .

In the type of broad and vigorous program which I have outlined there will be a constant temptation to ape the Russians in their tactics of subversive warfare and so-called "black" propaganda. Should we open an "Agit-Prop" school in Washington for our foreign sympathizers, training them in the tactics of infiltration, when to call a general strike, the technique of street fighting, what ministries to demand in a coalition government? Should we secretly finance undergrounds behind the Iron Curtain? Should we, through blinds and front organizations, surreptitiously buy and finance newspapers and radio stations abroad? No; in our hands such weapons would be self-defeating. They are useful in the power struggle only for the temporary seizure of power by a minority clique; they are effective only when seizure is consolidated by ruthless suppression and terror. Every step we take should be open, honest, identified, and to the fullest possible extent in cooperation with other governments.

Such a program as I have outlined has two great virtues. It is realistic, practical, hard-headed, and hard-boiled because it is pitched precisely at the central issue of our time—the worldwide struggle for the minds and loyalties of mankind. Thus it calls for weapons appropriate to such a struggle, not for the weapons of past wars. But above all, it calls for the mobilization of those elements in our life which most become us as men, the appeal to reason and truth. In the ultimate victory of such an appeal we can, because we are human in a world of humans, hold final confidence.

BASIC STRATEGY TO COUNTER THE BIG LIE [3]

The democracies must take the offensive in political warfare against the totalitarian regime of the Soviet Union and keep the

[3] From "To Counter the Big Lie—A Basic Strategy," by Sidney Hook, Professor of Philosophy, New York University. New York *Times Magazine*. p9+. March 11, 1951. Reprinted by permission.

offensive. But the strategy and tactics must be formulated differently for the different areas of conflict. . . .

Political warfare in Western European countries is of the very first importance in fanning the will to resist aggression. . . . Current political warfare in Western Europe is largely based on a truth campaign about the United States. Although a certain amount of information is necessary for political purposes, the emphasis is mistaken. What is required—primarily, if not exclusively—is the dissemination of truth, not so much about the United States as about the Soviet Union. . . .

Were a truth campaign about the Soviet Union waged in Western Europe and carried into every city and village square the moral position of the mass Communist parties of France and Italy would be strongly undermined because the latter have so closely identified themselves with the USSR. Nor should this campaign neglect to underscore the motives of extreme Russian nationalism behind Soviet international professions. As for other groups of the population . . . it is not hard to show that everyone has something to lose. . . .

In the satellite countries . . . political warfare . . . should pursue three tactically interrelated lines. The first must be the continuous assurance to the peoples suffering under the Communist yoke that they are not alone in their struggles, that the West has not forgotten them. . . . The second must suggest ways of continuous opposition to Communist rule. . . . The third, directed especially to the Communists among the satellite powers, should drive home the fact that their country is being systematically pillaged by the Soviet Union, their national interests betrayed, and their best traditions dishonored. . . .

All efforts of political warfare must be ultimately directed to weakening the Communist party dictatorship in the Soviet Union. For it is the head and fount of Communist opposition and aggression throughout the world. The most massive concentration of the weapons of propaganda and education should therefore be trained here and their contents carefully appraised.

For technical reasons, resulting from the regime's self-imposed cordon against the West and the stringency of its internal controls, the vast masses of the Russian people cannot be reached by political warfare. But we do know that the political propaganda directed *to* the Soviet Union, and the little circulated *within* it, is received primarily by Communist party officials and members in the multiform organizations in which they play the leading role. It is this fact which should determine the kind of political warfare we should wage in the USSR. . . .

The political strategy of our approach to those in the Soviet apparatus should be that Stalin and his lieutenants have betrayed all the principles of the October Revolution, wiped out its early progressive measures, liquidated the few remaining traces of democracy which existed in the first years. . . . To the extent that these men regard themselves as Marxists, we must contrast Marxist principles, especially where they promise freedom and speak about the dignity and independence of the worker, with current Soviet practices, and lay these practices squarely at Stalin's door. The theme song should be: What Marx (and even Lenin) proclaimed, Stalin has betrayed.

REACHING THE MASSES VIA TV [4]

The Advisory Commission on Information, in its March 1949 report to Congress, prefaced its conclusions with the following questions and answers:

Q. Is this program . . . effective? A. Yes; as far as it goes.

Q. Is it adequate? A. No.

In its report issued in September 1949, the Commission re-emphasized this point, saying: "The United States information program falls short of the effectiveness expected by Congress. . . ."

While . . . we are trying . . . to penetrate beyond the Iron Curtain to keep alive at least the feeble flame of hope . . . our present emphasis must be upon the human beings outside the Iron

[4] From "The Vision of America," remarks on the floor of the Senate by Karl E. Mundt of North Dakota. *Congressional Record.* 96:8130-9. June 5, 1950.

Curtain whose sympathetic adherence to either ideology is the goal of both contestants in this cold war. . . .

Two thirds of the world's population today is mostly illiterate. The life expectancy of this multitude of people is no more than 30 years. They live in regions without transportation or communications of any kind. Their mental processes have never been stimulated. Their lives are spent in search of a bare existence and the result of their insufferable toil is a diet of but 2,000 calories daily—hardly enough to support life. . . . These are the people . . . which both the Communists and those who oppose that godless tyranny are trying to reach if either side is to become dominant enough to prevent this cold war from growing into . . . a hot war. . .

It can easily be realized that our present information program is inadequate when it comes to this vast population because we do not and cannot reach these multitudes by present techniques. To these illiterates, all our libraries, bulletins, pamphlets, and publications are useless. Without radio receivers, even where our Voice of America broadcasts are adequate, such people cannot hear our message. Living in remote areas, far from accessible transportation, our information personnel are not able to contact them in significant numbers. . . .

The tragedy is that we have, as yet, never found the means to show them a way by which these people themselves can work their own way out of misery into a more fruitful life. We have extended money grants, most of which have never reached the people, and which certainly cannot help them to help themselves. The size of the problem and the scope of the challenge are so great that to try to meet the need by direct economic aid and assistance from the United States might well bankrupt this country before we could even make a significant change in the lives, environment, or attitudes of these backward multitudes.

Our problem, therefore, is to find a technique which will achieve this objective before these areas are taken over by the Communists, and one which can do so within the budgetary limitations of our own national resources and abilities. . . . We must add a practical and realistic approach to the minds and hearts of hundreds of millions of people whom we have been unable to contact, and whose standards of living are still so low that appeals must be based on a more pragmatic and immediate basis.

Let us accept as fact that the world recognizes that we have the "know-how." What it is looking for from us today is the "show-how." . . . To "show-how" means to cause something to be understood, and it means to make evident by demonstration. It intends that things be made visible. It recognizes that one picture is worth 10,000 words.

Most of us are just coming dimly to realize that the world is today entering a new era of show-how. . . . We recognize that a new medium of expression—television, mass sight coupled with hearing—has become a practical reality for us in America. What I now ask Senators to do is to . . . consider . . . whether it is possible to reach the masses outside the Soviet orbit by audio-video techniques. . . .

It is proposed that a television network be established at strategic points throughout the areas to be served. . . .

To insure satisfactory relay operations the stations forming links of the network chain would be 50 to 125 miles apart, at elevated points where strong signals could be received. Such a network would constitute a complete, integrated audio-video intercommunication system. . . . For example, a nationwide network in either Japan, Turkey, or Indonesia could be constructed for the estimated total cost of $4.6 million. These expenditures would be broken down as follows:

22 relay transmission stations (mountain-top) with equipment, including towers and Diesel generators, each at $150,000	$3,300,000
22 buildings to contain the foregoing, each at $30,000	660,000
Engineering and supervision of network construction	300,000
Completely equipped central studio	350,000
Total	$4,610,000

For a similar nationwide television network in the Philippines, the estimated cost of—

17 such relay stations (mountaintop) with full equipment, including towers and Diesel generators at $150,000 per unit	$2,550,000
17 buildings, each at $30,000	510,000
Engineering and supervision of network construction	250,000
Completely equipped central studios	350,000
Total	$3,660,000

I suggest that the only effective and feasible means today for "making available to peace-loving peoples the benefits of our store of technical knowledge, in order to help them realize their aspirations for a better life," as the State Department has proposed it for American consideration, is to show how our know-how is able to produce results.

I venture the belief that, with a well-conceived agricultural help program televised to farmers in foreign areas we could increase their farm output 10 per cent to 20 per cent in our first year of operation in any given area.

I want to make it clear, however, that at the same time farmers are being shown profitable agricultural procedures simultaneous urban audio-video demonstrations in public health, such as proper methods of child feeding and care, can be demonstrated on other transmission units. They can, of course, be orally related in the language or dialects of the particular area, tribe, or people. This is because the proposed communication network is a transmission-link system and, when the overall network is not in use, audio-video broadcasts can be made from any transmission unit, and the programs can be projected by speakers and demonstrators selected from the specific local areas to whom the educational programs are directed. Thus we entirely overcome our present language problems. . . .

This great television network program does not contemplate and it does not require the use of individual television receiver sets. . . . This plan will use community receiver sets such as are now available and such as are now in general use here in America. . . .

In summary, the system of telecommunication which I propose for suitable areas is a comprehensive one, including television. Such an overall system is a necessary arm of national life and welfare. Modern techniques make such a system practical and reasonable in initial cost, operation, and maintenance. A system with proper video programming promises national integration and progress and can build effective irreducible barriers against the march of Communism.

BLUEPRINT FOR PROPAGANDA TO EASTERN EUROPE [5]

Propaganda, whatever its nature, cannot by itself lead to the liberation of Eastern European peoples. . . . In modern times, no revolution against an established government has been the result of ideas alone, of truth alone. . . . Most of the modern revolutions . . . were actually carried out by organized social forces. And such organized forces . . . do not exist in Eastern Europe any more. . . .

Propaganda can make an essential contribution to the eventual liberation of Eastern Europe only if it is conceived as a means preparatory to action. What kind of action? Passive resistance in the first place and, in the second place, the sort of action which is already being undertaken on a worldwide scale by the Communists and which can be best described as subversive-unorthodox warfare. . . .

Let us turn to the content of broadcasts addressed to Eastern Europe. These should be aimed at stimulating the majorities with the future action in view and toward demoralizing and disrupting the ruling groups. Their first function is to create not only the hope but the certainty that Soviet communism will be defeated. The fundamental theme which cannot be too often re-

[5] From "Propaganda to Eastern Europe," by Brutus Coste, former member of the Rumanian diplomatic service and long-time student of Eastern European affairs. *Public Opinion Quarterly*. 14:629-66. Winter 1950-51. Reprinted by permission.

peated in the most varied form, from short editorials to talks by public leaders and historians, is the inevitability of the victory of freedom.

To make such a theme really convincing, constant stress should be laid upon the strength and the determination of the free world. News given in straight form should be selected carefully so as to convey this impression. Comments and talks on the international situation should unceasingly underscore such strength and determination. . . .

News reports and commentaries regarding the world situation should avoid representing Western policy in purely defensive terms. The fact that the Atlantic Pact has been discussed in such terms has had disheartening effects. It is quite understandable that such interpretations are given to Western Europe. When it comes, however, to propaganda addressed to Eastern Europe it would be essential to represent the Atlantic policy only as a necessary first step in a global policy aimed at the establishment of a free world. Such an interpretation would be more convincing if it were made clear that there is a new trend in Western policy, that there is no tendency over here to uphold in any way the policy of appeasement and its fruits. . . .

There are other . . . indirect means to foster faith in eventual liberation. The first of these is the frequent transmission of talks, statements, short comments and published reports that would show that despite Communist censorship the Western World knows and understands what is going on in Eastern Europe, and that it not only condemns the men responsible but keeps a record of their crimes for the day of retribution. . . .

It should be made clear that the free world keeps a full record of every good deed of any member of the ruling group. To make such warnings more effective, specific and otherwise unpublicized misdeeds, giving the names and positions of the individuals responsible for them, should be transmitted from time to time. This implies, of course, improved intelligence.

It is useless to transmit straight, uncommented news about events in Eastern European countries that are reported by the Communist press, such as changes in the personnel of the administrations, new laws, etc. It is harmful to report coldly the death and prison sentences given to brave patriots. Adequate words should be said to honor the peasant who has fallen in defense of his land, the guerilla fighter who died fighting or before a firing squad and the men and women sent to prison for their political ideas. It is not enough to deny the charges of espionage for some Western power brought against individuals or groups. Whenever reporting sentences brought against such men and women it should be stressed that their real guilt was their faith in freedom and in the right of their nation to live in freedom and independence. Any comment which is confined to the denial of charges of espionage often conveys the impression that brave people have been let down. In all such comments there should be a punch-line, a reference to future retribution.

Another indirect means of conveying a message of hope is to report the public activities of exiled leaders, as well as the activities of the American nationality groups on behalf of freedom for the Eastern European nations. Most letters from these countries urge that this be done more extensively, as it would give to the listeners the reassuring feeling that their case is being actively upheld.

Broadcasting can also help in creating a substitute for a free political life. If the exiled leaders were allowed to discuss over the radio the views of the political parties which they represent or their personal views with regard to the future political and economic reconstruction of our nations, the benefits would be twofold. In the first place the listeners would get another message of hope. The very fact that the practical problems of future reconstruction are being discussed, will be for them an indication that talk about eventual liberation represents more than empty words. In the second place, a very useful bit of political education would in this way be accomplished.

In addition to discussions of the future reconstruction, such programs should also comprise talks by Americans or exiles on the philosophy of democracy, on the practical working of democracy in America and Western Europe, and on the current literature dealing with these subjects. Programs of this kind would enable the peoples of Eastern Europe to think, in full possession of the facts, about the problems which they themselves will have to solve one day. . . .

It is, of course, not necessary that those discussing the domestic problems of Eastern Europe be in entire agreement. There will be a common ground: the fundamental philosophy of democracy which is accepted in the Western world from the non-Communist left to the conservative right. But within this limitation, there should be freedom to express any opinion on the political, economic and social reconstruction of Eastern Europe.

There are two more types of morale-sustaining broadcasts which deserve mention. Eastern Europeans have strong religious feelings. Therefore, no Sunday or religious holiday should be allowed to pass without at least a prayer for their liberation, a prayer to appeal to all religious faiths. From time to time, sermons could be given by ministers of the various religious denominations represented in the satellite countries. These too should inspire hope in a better tomorrow.

On the other hand, nothing is more effective in lowering Communist prestige and Communist claims of successful accomplishments than ridicule and satire. It would be good for the oppressed and would demoralize at least some of the oppressors. Therefore satire and humor, always with a political tinge, should be regular fare on the radio. . . .

The greatest assets of Soviet propaganda are certain facts that seem to be speaking louder than words. It is obvious that in the present world situation, pending the consolidation of the West, the free world will hardly be able to create dramatic facts that would match Soviet political successes in recent years. There are, however, certain facts that can be created and advertised effectively.

The Western World in general and the United States in particular could set up and operate a program of practical training for young refugees from Eastern Europe. The United States and to some extent Great Britain could concentrate on training men in the various branches of central and local government, in production, in modern business management, in public works, labor relations, public welfare and education; France could take care of the artists, educators and jurists; Denmark and Holland could train experts in agriculture and farmers' cooperatives. The yearly cost of such a program for 600 young Eastern Europeans would be less than two million dollars.

Such action would yield tremendous eventual benefits. If rightly advertised in Eastern Europe, it would also bring immediate returns. To be able to tell Eastern Europe and the world at large that while the Soviets have been and are training agents of destruction, the Western World is engaged in the training of men who would eventually carry the spirit, knowledge, and experience of the free world to the underdeveloped nations of Eastern Europe would not only be a profitable propaganda move but, above all else, a genuine act of faith in the future of democratic government.

Secondly, with the termination of IRO [the International Refugee Organization] there will be no organization able to take care of the yet unsettled refugees from Eastern Europe and of those, ever less numerous, who can make an escape. It should be possible to work out some means of assuring to at least recently escaped refugees the chance to work for a living. Only the knowledge of such action can successfully counteract the depressing effect of Soviet propaganda regarding Western indifference.

Another function of Western propaganda should be that of helping Eastern European peoples preserve their traditional Western and national values; spiritual, moral, intellectual and artistic. . . . There should, in the first place, be regular talks by noted Western thinkers and writers on the spiritual values of free men, in contract to the cynical and unscientifically dogmatic materialism of communism.

There should also be regular courses on the traditional ethical concepts of these peoples and on their history. The latter, while correcting the distortions of Communist writers of "history," should depart, however, in some respects, from the traditional line of many of our Eastern European historians. . . . The broadcasts on history should . . . contain no derogatory statements about any of these nations; no expressions of hatred, no underestimation of these nations' past, of their achievements and character; they should play down past differences and stress common traits and interests. Within such limitations, no holiday or any important anniversary should pass without adequate commemorations.

There should be regular, at least fortnightly, lectures on all Eastern European languages. In such lectures the Communist tendency of distorting the most precious heritage should be counteracted not only with the weapon of linguistics, but also with that of ridicule. There should be lectures on, and readings from, Eastern classics and those silenced writers whose writings are being shamelessly falsified to suit the Communist line. It would be a great comfort for these people to learn that while suppressed at home, their true national culture survives in the free world. For this purpose the cultural activities of exiled artists, scientists and educators should be carefully reported. Their writings should be reviewed and excerpts read from them, particularly from writings and poetry extolling the heroism of resistance fights or expressing faith in the resurrection of the various nations.

The third function of broadcasting is, in my judgment, the furtherance of a sentiment of solidarity and of confidence among the non-Communist majorities, for such sentiment is prerequisite to future action. . . . The most effective way to do this is to stress by frequent talks on the subject the fact that communism is at war with all democratic ideas, with all religious denominations, with all the races inhabiting the occupied lands, with all the sections of society which have been turned into slaves of Moscow and its puppets. There should be frequent exhortations to brotherhood. These should come, when possible, from religious leaders, Western and national, of the denominations represented in each country; from exiled members of racial minorities; from genuine representatives, Western and national, of the various sections of society. Let labor leaders and rank-and-file workers speak to the working class, farmers speak to the peasants, professional people to doctors, lawyers, and technicians, women to women, young men to youth. . . .

The fourth task that broadcasting can serve is the fostering of a regionwide solidarity and a feeling that these peoples belong to free Europe and will ultimately regain a place in the European community.

There is today an inarticulate awareness that purely national solutions cannot protect Eastern Europe against the recurrence of the tragedy which has been its lot not only in the past ten years, but during the greater part of its history. This awareness has to be fostered and made more articulate. Any effort in this direction would bring benefits not only after liberation, but would also make for synchronized action when the time for action comes, since it would make people conscious of the strength of over 80 million people who are morally united.

The means to this end are numerous: reports on the common efforts of the exiled leaders; talks by these leaders on the common interests of their people and on the necessity of building a powerful federation that would assure them a long period of peace in which to develop cultural and economic potentialities; talks on the advantages of joining a European federation, when and if such a federation should take shape. Such talks would have to stress that an Eastern European federation will be established even if Western Europe has not merged by the time liberation is a fact. The new approach in the teaching of history with which I have already dealt can greatly assist in such efforts, as would reports on any plans of federation worked out, in common, by exiles from these lands.

USING COMMUNIST TACTICS AGAINST RUSSIA [6]

Russia's downfall could be gotten ready by the use of three instruments: (1) political warfare, (2) "white" psychological warfare, and (3) "black" psychological warfare. Political warfare consists of the use of politics to supplement the winning of war or to achieve purposes comparable to those usually accomplished by war. White psychological warfare is the term for propaganda carried on in the open. Black psychological

[6] From "Hotfoot for Stalin," by Paul M. A. Linebarger, Professor of Asiatic Politics, School of Advanced International Studies, Johns Hopkins University. *Nation's Business*. 39:29-31+. April 1951. Reprinted by permission.

warfare is the trade name for secret propaganda, waged either by disguised agents or by other clandestine means.

What could we accomplish with $500 million spent on black operations directed against Russia and her satellites? . . . For $500 million plus enthusiasm . . . we could launch a massive and terrifying campaign of political, white and black psychological warfare, and some economic warfare against Moscow. Even if we did not stop Russian aggression for the time being, we could cause it to falter. By taking the offensive we could make the USSR and its satellites spend big money in meeting our small money. Increased police measures, lower economic production, higher defense budgets, greater security expenditure, wider and more wasteful deployment of troops and police—these would be some of the initial results of Americans giving a hot-foot to the Politburo.

Political warfare could support anti-Soviet governments-in-exile for all the Iron Curtain countries. Take one example. The world needs a democratic Russian Government very badly. Obviously such a government cannot be set up in Russia in the face of millions of informers, spies, militarized and special police, but an anti-Stalin government could easily be set up outside of Russia. Even if Russia's seat in the United Nations were not given to the new government, it could at least send its own delegation to protest in proper form every time Stalin's delegate opened his mouth. The Russians themselves have a case against Stalin, and if they know that others outside of Russia are encouraged to work for their liberation, we may get a real reaction. . . .

Along with prodemocratic governments, we could help set up friendly armies from the Iron Curtain countries. We would challenge the Reds with the presence of a liberation force which might be turned against them and set up a way to support those who escape from Communist dictatorships. . . .

Another technique consists of splitting the Communists apart from each other. Tito already has broken loose from the dictatorship of Moscow. . . . Perhaps it is not too late to help turn the Chinese Communists against Moscow. Communist leaders both big and little break away in the satellite countries almost every week. Country by country the United States would have a major decision to make. . . .

In Burma, India, and Ceylon there are rebellious factions of the Communist movement; in Hungary, Bulgaria and Czechoslovakia there were. The Communist schismatics in Eastern Europe did not, with the exception of Tito, obtain our effective help in time to stay alive. In many situations we might find it necessary to support secretly or openly both the anti-Communists and the schismatic Communists for the time being.

White psychological warfare could take the form of the Voice of America, for example. The *Daily Worker* is an example from the Russian side. In each case the source of propaganda is what it professes to be. This type of warfare can supplement subversion. It can encourage the overthrow of dictatorships. It can promise a point of refuge. It can boast about the clandestine operations without giving them away. . . .

Black psychological warfare would involve either Americans or anti-Stalin Russians publishing underground newspapers within Russia. Combined with political warfare, it would attempt to organize Russian intellectuals, technicians, workers, and peasants into conspiratorial groups designed to overthrow Stalin with or without the help of the United Nations or American armed forces, when the time came for Russia's liberation. . . . Black psychological warfare could do to Russia exactly what she is doing to America, while giving the Politburo no more legal ground for war against us than we already have for war against international communism.

Finally, economic warfare techniques would supplement these other open, semisecret, and secret methods of attack-short-of-war. The Russians are known to have printed excellent counterfeits of United States currency. They are known to have sabotaged factories, to have encouraged the destruction of raw material, to have promoted economic chaos within non-Soviet countries. . . . There is no trick in the whole Communist arsenal of subversion which we could not match if we decided to do so.

Such a program could start with $500 million. That amount spent on ordinary weapons will produce three divisions at the front; with economies it might produce five or six. But $500 million for subversion would have the effect on communism of at least 30 American divisions.

THE IMMEDIATE PROBLEM [7]

[Recently] 28 Senators asked President Truman to open, by a great expansion of United States propaganda facilities, a psychological and spiritual offensive against the Kremlin. . . .

If we in the United States were exceedingly successful in reaching and influencing the Russian people today, in our very success there might be an element of danger for the people of the United States. The Russian rulers, like all rulers all through history, would vastly prefer a foreign war to a civil or domestic war. The success of our efforts in stirring up the Russian people today to the kind of revolt which we may perhaps hope is ultimately indicated within that country and by that great people could invite their autocratic rulers who have complete control of the Russian armies into open assault against Western Europe.

I suggest to the Senate that the urgent and immediate problem today is not the hard core of Russia. The real problem is on the outside, and we should be working from the outside inward, instead of from the inside outward. Let us start with the free peoples of the world themselves. We now have an example in South Korea. A recent poll in South Korea showed that one third of the South Koreans thought that they indeed did attack the North Koreans. Here we see the power of the big lie as reiterated in the Soviet propaganda. We have plenty of evidence of the need with the French people.

REDEFINITION OF AIMS [8]

In formulating American propaganda, it is essential, first, to define the values we consider most important for export under a

[7] From remarks on the floor of the Senate by Senator William Benton of Connecticut. *Congressional Record*. 96:13086. August 21, 1950.

[8] From "What Should U.S. Information Policy Try to Do?" by Vera M. Dean, editor. *Foreign Policy Bulletin*. 29:3-4. March 31, 1950. Reprinted by permission.

"Marshall Plan in the field of ideas"; and, second, to assess the impression our values will make on other peoples. This twofold task is complicated by genuine and legitimate divergences among ourselves as to the ideas we want to promote and see adopted abroad. All of us stress our wide range of freedoms. . . . Most of us pay at least lip-service to racial equality and nondiscrimination—although recognizing the gap that still separates reality from the idea.

In the economic and social field divergences are sharper. Some of us recognize the extent to which the concept of free enterprise has been gradually modified here by voluntary acceptance of various forms of governmental intervention in economic life. Others consider socialism of the British type a stage in transition to communism, or even identical with communism, and yearn to abolish both. Some see no viable alternative to communism in backward areas except a program of reforms that would strike at the roots of ancient and modern maladjustments. Others, fearful of change here, sometimes consciously, but most often unconsciously, want to defend the *status quo* abroad.

Which of these diverse schools of thought represents the opinions of the majority of the American people? Who is to decide this in elaborating the propaganda program of the United States? Would it be advisable for the American people to make themselves heard directly—not merely through official presentations—in other nations? And is there a way of doing it?

But even after we have answered these questions, we still must discover how our ideas affect peoples abroad. What impression, for example, do we make in Britain and other strongly Socialist countries of Europe by denouncing socialism? A. A. Berle, Jr., former Assistant Secretary of State, a non-Socialist well known for his opposition to communism, believes our failure to realize that "outside the Iron Curtain, organized socialism is a major non-Communist force" constitutes "the blunder that may destroy the West." But "the demonstrable fact," Mr. Berle contends, "is that Socialist governments and parties do not lead towards a Communist state."

While promoting our own ideas abroad, we need to develop at least as much patience with the imperfections of others as we hope to enlist for our own. We are entitled to insist on the desirability of free elections, provided we understand why less advanced peoples have not reached our stage of political maturity, just as we ourselves plead for time in the realization of our racial ideals when taken to task on this score by critics abroad. It is legitimate for us to criticize the imperialist practices of all nations, whether democracies like Britain and France or Communist dictatorships like Russia. But our criticisms will sound more convincing abroad if we do not take over, on the plea of self-defense, some of the obligations of colonial powers, as in the case of Indo-China. We are within our rights to reject planned economy if we think that is the thing to do. But we shall be accused of double-talk if at the same time we urge the Marshall Plan nations to hasten their integration—a goal which calls for a great deal of economic planning. . . .

[The] mental gulf between us and other peoples . . . cannot be successfully closed with Fourth-of-July platitudes about democracy. Nor can it be closed, as in time of war, by dramatic appeals to other peoples to hit specified targets—unless we decide to use psychological warfare measures to foment revolutions in Russia and neighboring countries. If we are aiming not at short-term victories but at a long-term program, we may benefit by General Eisenhower's advice in his address of March 24 on "Implementing the Peace of the World":

> There is no need to remake the world, outside the Soviet system, in the likeness of the United States or any other country. What I do suggest is that we recognize that every culture developed in the world has been worked out by its possessors to meet the circumstances of their own environment. Each race and each nation can learn from every other. There is none so close to self-sufficiency that it can do without the help and cooperation of others; none so primitive that it has not amassed a wisdom that can possibly enlighten even the most advanced.

A MORAL CRUSADE [9]

The only possible way to secure a world of true peace and justice is by taking men away from Stalin and the Cominform leaders and winning them over to our side.

[9] From "We Can Pierce the Iron Curtain," by Brien McMahon, Senator from Connecticut, chairman of the Joint Congressional Committee on Atomic Energy. New York *Times Magazine*. p7+. June 24, 1951. Reprinted by permission.

Three facts are fundamental in this struggle for the hearts and loyalties of men. *Fact one* is that behind the Iron Curtain untold millions now actually believe the monstrous calumnies of the Politburo; they actually think that Stalin stands for peace and we stand for war. *Fact two* is that the Iron Curtain conceals profound discontent among the ordinary peoples of the Soviet empire. . . . *Fact three* is that we have it within our power to pierce the Iron Curtain with a bold and constructive program for peace—a program that can convert the peoples of the Soviet empire into actual or potential allies. Even our present very modest information program is reaching millions in the Soviet Union and its satellite states. The Kremlin's all-out jamming campaign against Voice of America broadcasts is in itself proof of the infectiousness of our idea of liberty—and Stalin's mortal fear of the truth.

It is paradoxical that those who have spoken most loudly about the world's misunderstanding of American motives are frequently the same people who have obstructed every effort to make the truth about ourselves known. Truth, we should know by now, is not self-propagating.

It will take large outlays of money to run a campaign of truth comparable in magnitude to the Soviet's campaign of lies. The $115 million that the State Department has recently requested for its information program is by no means excessive. I think, in fact, that this sum is far too small.

The technical problem of getting our message through the Iron Curtain is as challenging as any ever faced by experts in mass communication. We are dealing with an enemy who will stop at nothing to keep the truth from the Russian and satellite peoples. Should we, for instance, attempt to send leaflet-carrying balloons behind the Iron Curtain the Kremlin might employ hideous techniques to turn this campagn to its own advantage. It might have trusted party members booby-trap captured balloons and then turn these loose on an unsuspecting populace. It might manufacture copies of our balloons and impregnate these imitations with toxic agents.

Much, however, can be done. Major improvements in our Voice of America transmission facilities are already in prospect.

Testimony before the Senate Foreign Relations Committee—a large part of it necessarily classified—has revealed that the coming months will see a far higher proportion of our programs getting through the Soviet's jamming apparatus.

Yet I do not believe we can be content with this. I think we should immediately ask the United Nations to assert its right to operate its own radio station within the Soviet Union. I am not naive enough to suppose that Stalin will rush to accept such a proposal. However . . . if it is rejected, it will glaringly expose the sham and duplicity of Vishinsky's utterances.

Getting our radio signals into the Communist heartland is of little use if our potential audience does not have the means of receiving them. The great majority of the Iron Curtain peoples do not now own radios. But experts say that simple portable radios capable of picking up Voice programs can be made for as little as $2. If this can be done, I would propose manufacturing such sets by the million and shipping them to distribution depots in hundreds of cities around the border of Stalin's empire. . . .

People-to-people contact is the best possible antidote for misunderstanding. Those American soldiers who met the Soviet armies on the Elbe in 1945 will remember how continuing association gradually turned the distrust of many of the Russian soldiers into friendship. . . . Acquaintance with free men was so corrupting, in fact, that the Kremlin prevented mass desertions only by hurriedly rotating its occupation troops home.

I believe that the men of our veterans' organizations should now formally—and repeatedly—ask Stalin to let them again meet face to face with Soviet veterans—with the rank and file Russians who fought so valiantly against the legions of nazism. Let us see if Stalin will allow these men to visit in our cities and towns, and if he will allow our veterans in Russian homes. So, also, might our trade unions now request that the Kremlin allow American machinists and carpenters to visit the mills and homes of Stalingrad and Kiev, and that, in turn, Soviet workers be permitted to see at first hand the automobiles and gardens of the typical American workers in Detroit or Omaha. Our teachers' associations might issue a similar request—imagine what would happen if Soviet educators could witness our democratic school system in action.

I am not at all sure that Stalin would comply with such requests—but I am sure that people cannot be fooled forever. If Stalin ignores such patently reasonable proposals, if he refuses to let our people speak directly with the Russian people, Soviet citizens will eventually learn the meaning of these refusals.

No suggestion for breaching the curtain should be dismissed merely because it seems novel. I understand it is quite feasible to compile the names and addresses of a large number of Soviet citizens. I wonder whether our fraternal and professional organizations, our labor unions, our church groups and even our school children might not see fit to secure such lists and embark on a massive letter-writing campaign to the men and women of Odessa and Smolensk and Vladivostok. The Soviet censors, of course, would do their best to confiscate these letters. But such a spontaneous outpouring of sentiment from everyday Americans might well corrupt even the censors themselves.

There are many ways of making a censor's lot an unhappy one. It is well known that the Soviet Government makes strenuous efforts to secure almost all important American scientific journals. Soviet scientists and engineers are omnivorous readers of these publications. Our scientific and technical societies might be well advised to interlard their journals with discussions of topics such as academic freedom.

Nor should we ignore the possibility of mailing millions of mail-order catalogues to the Iron Curtain countries. Nothing can more tellingly refute lies about America's impoverishment than the consumers' wonderland contained within the pages of a Sears-Roebuck or a Montgomery Ward catalog.

In many cases we can best reach the Russian people through Soviet nationals now living outside the USSR. Hundreds of thousands of Russian soldiers are stationed in Eastern Europe. These troops can still be reached with the printed word. There is a real opportunity to take advantage of the extraordinary desertion rate among them. At the very least, we can make sure that those men who reluctantly return to the Soviet Union carry with them the germ of the idea of freedom.

Above all, we should support those brave political exiles who have risked their lives to flee their homeland and continue the fight against the Kremlin from the West. These men and women are publishing information bulletins, maintaining underground liaison with their home countries and actively aiding additional liberty-lovers to escape. They constitute the potential "cadres of liberation." Many of them are willing to risk torture and death by clandestinely returning to Russia.

It has been suggested that we establish a University of the Free, which would serve as a focal point for the activities of these political exiles. This makes sense. Such a university, which could draw its student body from young refugees, would have an enormous symbolic effect. It would be a sign that the West had not abandoned the Soviet and satellite peoples to Kremlin tyranny.

The cumulative result of injections of truth into the Soviet body politic will be far greater than many of us imagine. Lacking official and overt channels for disseminating the truth, the Russian people have developed the world's most elaborate news grapevine. A rumor first heard in Moscow in the morning is repeated in Leningrad the same evening; a few days later the same story is known in Vladivostok. Only one person on a collective farm may see a resistance pamphlet, or hear a Voice of America program, but the truth he learns may eventually become known to hundreds, or even thousands of Russians.

The problem of means—how to get the ear of the Russian and satellite peoples—should not be minimized. Yet the primary problem is that of ends—the point of the message we hope to get across.

What is it that we want to tell the world? Certain things seem clear. Our message must be based on the hard rock of truth. There is no place in our program for half truths, for clever verbal forays intended merely to score some embarrassing propaganda victory against the Kremlin. It is likewise apparent that our efforts must not be negative or defensive. Vital as it is to expose Stalin's falsehoods, we must guard against endless " 'tis-'taint" refutations of Moscow's fabrications. Nor should we dissipate our energies through an ever-changing "shotgun" type of appeal that does not really acquaint the world with the basic principles for which we stand.

Our campaign of truth must have a single theme of such motive force that it cannot fail to gain supporters. This theme must be appealing to men of all walks of life and all nations; it must be congenial equally to the ordinary Russians, the average Chinese and the rank and file Poles.

All decent men hate war and long for peace with justice—they want freedom from the fear of mass annihilation. All men want relief from poverty and disease—they want an end to the crushing burden of armaments expenditures; they would rejoice if men could instead join in a common fight against human wretchedness. The everyday peoples behind the Iron Curtain wish to live and let live; not to kill and be killed.

The Kremlin has brilliantly recognized—and unscrupulously exploited—these elementary truths. Although it is solely Communist imperialism that threatens the peace, the Kremlin has nevertheless posed as the prime defender of the peace. Although Stalin has ruthlessly stripped the satellite nations of their industries and resources, he claims to have the solution for depressions and poverty.

Yet the propaganda successes of the Kremlin give some measure of the victory that would be ours were we able to turn Stalin's own arguments against him. If we can show the world's peoples that we stand for justice and Stalin stands for tyranny; that we stand for bread and he stands for bombs; that we stand for peace and he stands for war; that we stand for life and he stands for death—if we can bring these truths home to all men, we can deprive Stalin of one thing he needs for conquest—the support of people.

This end will be in sight when the world is convinced of two things. First, that on the issue of peace and good will toward all decent people, we Americans stand as one man. Second, that we have a real program for achieving peace—not the peace that merely means absence of war but peace with justice, peace with abundance.

I therefore propose that this nation immediately launch a great moral crusade for peace akin in universality and appeal to the Fourteen Points and the Four Freedoms.

APPENDIX

NEWS HANDLING BY THE VOA: STORY OF MacARTHUR'S REMOVAL FROM FAR EASTERN COMMAND

The biggest news story of 1951 was General Douglas MacArthur's removal from command of the UN forces in Korea and of United States forces in the Far East. The problem of presenting this highly controversial issue to the peoples of the world was one to tax the most astute propagandist. Therefore, as an illustration of the United States information program's operation in the news field, a summary of news output for the three days following announcement of MacArthur's removal is reported here. Based on data received from the Office of International Information, this report includes summaries of news coverage of the Department's *Wireless Bulletin* for April 11-13, 1951, and excerpts from basic Voice of America scripts in English for the same period.

The *Wireless Bulletin* is prepared by the International Press and Publications Division of the Office of International Information. According to the letter transmitting copies of the *Bulletin* by O. C. Anderson, Director, Office of International Information, to the author, the *Bulletin*

> is sent daily to United States Information Officers abroad for distribution to foreign press agencies, to newspapers, foreign government officials and to other prominent persons who are in a position to influence public opinion abroad. The role of the *Wireless Bulletin* is to provide information to other countries about the official acts and pronouncements of the United States Government and the international organizations in which this country participates. Our Public Affairs Officers throughout the world select material from the *Wireless Bulletin* to be translated and distributed in the country to which they are assigned. Their decisions in this regard are based upon local needs and customs, foreign policy objectives of the United States and the extent to which the English language is spoken in a given area. Wireless bulletins transmitted by Morse code or by radio teletype, are monitored by approximately 70 of our diplomatic missions which air mail them to other missions not having reception facilities.

On April 11, 1951, *Wireless Bulletin No. 89* comprised 16 pages, 14½ of which dealt with various phases of the MacArthur story. The remaining 1½ pages dealt with estimates of enemy strength in Korea, the announcement of the ordering of an additional division of United States troops to Europe, and a story on Ambassador Dulles' return to Japan for peace talks.

On the following day, April 12, *Wireless Bulletin No. 90* totaled 15 pages, only five pages of which concerned the MacArthur story. Three of these five were devoted to President Truman's foreign policy address on Korea (which included the administration stand on the MacArthur "firing") and one of the other two pages referring to MacArthur dealt with General Ridgway's assumption of command. The remaining 10 pages of the *Bulletin* included the following items:

General U. S. News
- "Truman Starts Seventh Year in White House" .... 2p.
- "Dr Bunche Receives 1951 'Four Freedoms Award' " ...... ½p.
- "Racial Segregation Voted Out of Draft Measure" .... ½p.
- "State Department's Bureau of Economic Affairs Reorganized" .... ½p.

Labor—U. S.
- "Progress Made Toward Reestablishing Wage Board" .... ½p.

ECA News
- "European Defense Orders Given Priority Ratings" .... ½p.

General International
- "Proposal for Opium Production Control Opposed by Soviet, Poland" .... ½p.
- "Swedish Economist Heads International Monetary Fund" .... ½p.
- "Four Power Deputies Conference: Free Nations Will Hold to Defense Policies" .... 2p.

United Nations News
- "Those Who Weaken UN Not Seeking Peace: Lie" .... 1½p.
- "UN Members to Be Asked for Report on Troop Offers" 1p.

The April 13 release of the *Bulletin* (No. 91), centered most of its attention in 14 pages to United States policy abroad. The MacArthur incident was covered with 2½ pages of press editorial comment from across the nation on Truman's foreign policy speech of the 11th, 1½ pages devoted to United States policy toward Formosa, and 2¾ pages specifically dealing with MacArthur. The remaining pages of the April 13 *Bulletin* covered the following:

General U.S. News
- "Nation Honors Flier for Attempt to Rescue Negro Fellow Pilot" .... 1p.
- "Greece, Argentina Get Vessels from U. S." .... ½p.

Labor—U. S.
- "Major U. S. Labor Groups to Take Part in ILO Conference" .... ½p.

ECA News
- "Marshall Plan Nations Attract American Tourists" .... ½p.

General International
- "Ethiopia Sending Battalion of Troops to Korea" .... 1p.

United Nations News

"Lie Confident Yugoslavia Will Support Peace Effort" .... ½p.
"Trusteeship Council Aids Peace" .... ½p.
"Security Council to Take Up Israel-Syria Dispute" .... ½p.
"Wool Committee Moves to Speed Operations" .... ½p.
"U. S., UN Seek to Keep Korean War from Spreading: Warren Austin" .... 1¼p.

Judging from material supplied the author by the Office of International Information, Voice of America coverage of the MacArthur story was thorough and objective. In the 39 Voice of America news scripts studied, totaling 84 pages of copy, there was no evidence of "slanting" or "withholding" news of the controversy. While perhaps some of the "straight news" handling tended to emphasize the administration stand, extremely thorough coverage of the reactions of Congress and American and foreign radio and press was evident throughout. On the first day, April 11, for example, in 12 scripts, covering nearly 36 pages of news material, only 6½ pages were "straight news" on the event, another six pages included the text of Truman's foreign policy address (including a short version), with the remaining copy dealing with congressional comment, roundups of American press and radio reaction, and the first reactions from foreign capitals.

Reproduced here are three sample scripts prepared on April 11, 1951. At a glance it can be seen that their handling of the news resembles closely that of any domestic radio station. *VOA 15* offers an example of a quarter-hour newscast, while *VOB 11* (prepared for the French desk) illustrates the handling of one phase of the story for a specific target area. *VOA 62* has been reproduced in part only, to show the use of *optional* material which might have the effect of "slanting" the news to some degree.

These scripts are basic English-language scripts, prepared by the Department of State's International Broadcasting Division in New York. They are used by Voice of America "country specialists" as the basic material from which foreign language scripts are prepared, according to Mr. Anderson, director of OII [Office of International Information], in his letter to the author. He said further:

> All broadcast material is cleared prior to use by officers who insure that the substance of the translated material does not deviate from the Department's policy guidances which are furnished to writers and translators in order to insure that United States foreign policy objectives are correctly interpreted in our radio, press and film programs.

Unfortunately, copies of such guidances governing handling of the MacArthur story are not available for security reasons. However, a sample guidance released by the congressional committee investigating United States foreign policy recently is reproduced. This should provide some idea of the basis of news treatment on the Voice of America.

VOA 15: QUARTER HOUR NEWSCAST, 4/11/51

1. Washington—President Truman early today relieved General Douglas MacArthur of his Far East commands. Lieutenant General Matthew Ridgway, Commander of UN Ground Forces in Korea, was named to succeed him. Lieutenant General James Van Fleet will replace General Ridgway. The changes are effective immediately.

2. The President said he made the change with deep regret but had concluded that General MacArthur "is unable to give his wholehearted support to the policies of the United States Government and of the United Nations in matters pertaining to his official duties."

3. The move made it clear that there is no change in United States foreign policy.

4. General MacArthur has indicated disagreement with the administration's Far Eastern policy a number of times in recent months. His statements were climaxed last week in a letter to Republican Representative Joseph Martin in which General MacArthur supported suggestions for use of Chinese Nationalist troops on the China mainland and declared that Asia is the main battlefield in the struggle against communism.

5. President Truman in his statement today noted that "full and vigorous debate on matters of national policy is a vital element in the constitutional system of our free democracy."

6. But at the same time, President Truman pointed out that military commanders "must be governed by the policies and directives issued to them in the manner provided by our laws and Constitution."

7. President Truman paid full tribute to General MacArthur's "distinguished services to the nation" and said his place in history is fully established. The President's statement came at an unusual White House news conference at one o'clock in the morning, Washington time. The statement was released to coincide with delivery of the orders to General MacArthur in Tokyo.

8. The appointment of General Ridgway to replace MacArthur brings a veteran combat soldier to command of the UN campaign against Communist aggression in Korea. General Ridgway assumed command of the Eighth Army after the death of Lieutenant General Walton Walker last December 23rd.

9. In his new post, General Ridgway will assume all four of General MacArthur's commands: Supreme Commander Allied Powers, United Nations Commander, Commander in Chief Far East, and Commanding General, United States Army Far East.

10. General Ridgway's successor as UN Ground Commander, General Van Fleet, is another outstanding American combat veteran.

General Van Fleet is former Chief of the American Military Mission in Greece.

11. There is still no official reaction from Tokyo. Dispatches said General MacArthur received word of the decision during the afternoon and soon after went to his headquarters, where he turned over his duties to his Chief of Staff. An aide said there would be no immediate comment.

12. Correspondents in Korea said the news was received with complete surprise at General Ridgway's headquarters. General Ridgway was on a tour of UN units with Army Secretary Frank Pace when word of his new appointment was received from Washington. He reportedly will leave for Tokyo immediately. General Van Fleet who is now in the United States is expected to leave for the Korean Front within a few days. Lieutenant General Frank Milburn will serve as Commander of the Eighth Army until General Van Fleet arrives.

13. Reaction to the presidential announcement developed quickly in many parts of the world.

14. In Washington, initial reaction divided along political lines. Republicans generally criticized the President's move while Democrats came to his support. Observers predicted a sharp political controversy in the days ahead over both the change in General MacArthur's status and the administration's Far East policy.

15. Republican Senator Robert Taft called the decision a "tragic error." He was joined in his criticism by Republican Senators Kenneth Wherry, William Knowland, Bourke Hickenlooper, Joseph McCarthy and Homer Ferguson. But at least one Republican, Senator James Duff of Pennsylvania, said "If this is the only way to get unity it must be done."

16. Democratic comment stressed the point that the President took the step in the interests of national security. Senator Robert Kerr like a number of other spokesmen regretted the necessity of the decision but supported the President's move.

17. Earle Cocke, Commander of the American Legion, the nation's largest veterans' organization, said he did not approve of the move but emphasized that President Truman was acting within his rights. He appealed to all Americans "to join in giving the men fighting in Korea and their new commander, their utmost support."

18. At Lake Success, United Nations delegates declined official comment except to endorse the appointment of General Ridgway. Both General Assembly President Nasrollah Entezam and acting Secretary General Konstantin Zinchenko refused to give any comment. A number of delegates said that the announcement came as a complete surprise.

19. Other United Nations sources explained that President Truman had complete authority to relieve General MacArthur as UN Commander. The Security Council resolution authorizing a UN command in Korea designated the United States as the agent to conduct the

campaign and General MacArthur was named to the post by President Truman.

20. In Britain, government and opposition leaders also withheld comment although Foreign Minister Herbert Morrison is expected to give official reaction to the change in a scheduled statement to Parliament on the situation in Korea.

21. At the Hague, the Netherlands Government authorized an official statement praising the "outstanding military capacities of General MacArthur." The statement added: "but recently the Netherlands Government has become more and more concerned about his public statements. The Netherlands Government believes that President Truman's action in replacing him was a wise one."

22. In Italy, Premier Alcide De Gasperi said through a spokesman: "We hope that what must have been a difficult and painful decision will prove to have been a contribution to peace by alleviating world tension."

23. In Paris and Copenhagen, newspapers editorially supported the move. Former French Premier Paul Reynaud said "Mr. Truman's decision solves an American problem and an inter-allied issue."

24. The French Press Agency said: "Diplomatic circles realized perfectly that the United States Government's policy in the Far East profoundly opposed General MacArthur's hazardous initiatives but they also realize how painful it was for President Truman to make this decision against a great soldier with a glorious past and a renowned name. . . . The decision could not have given more eloquent proof that the United States and its Allies desire peace."

25. UN Secretary General Trygve Lie, who is now in Paris, refused to comment.

26. In Tokyo, Lieutenant General Sir Horace Robertson, Australian Commander of the British Commonwealth Occupation Forces in Japan, publicly thanked General MacArthur for his great services in World War II and the United Nations action in Korea. He also welcomed the appointment of General Ridgway.

27. In Manila, where General MacArthur served for many years, Philippine legislators expressed their admiration for the General and said the struggle against communism must continue.

28. In India, Prime Minister Jawaharlal Nehru refused to make immediate comment.

29. Here are some other late reactions from around the world:

30. A French Foreign Office spokesman said that the decision showed that the United States and its Allies want to solve world problems peacefully, not only in Korea but also in Europe.

31. In Italy, Foreign Minister Carlo Sforza said President Truman's decision guarantees that there will be only one policy in the Far East—that of the United Nations.

32. There has been no comment from Communist regimes as yet. TASS is reported to have carried a brief story on the announcement. And the East German Press has carried the news without comment.

VOB 11: SPECIAL STORY FOR FRENCH DESK

1. Tokyo: General Douglas MacArthur received word of removal from all his Far Eastern commands while entertaining guests at luncheon at his home. The official orders in which President Truman relieved General MacArthur came a few minutes after a radio broadcast had announced the news.

2. Major General Courtney Whitney, military secretary of the United Nations command, said General MacArthur took the news with soldierly stoicism. The secretary said "he never turned a hair . . . his soldierly qualities were never more pronounced."

3. General MacArthur had no immediate comment. After luncheon he spent three and a half hours in final conferences with his chief aides. He then returned to his home in the American Embassy. As President Truman's orders called for General MacArthur's immediate removal, his Chief of Staff, Major General Doyle Hickey, temporarily assumed command until the arrival of Lieutenant General Matthew Ridgway who will succeed General MacArthur.

VOA 62: SPECIAL NEWS EXCERPT

1. (Undated) President Truman's order today relieving General Douglas MacArthur of his Far East commands has stirred up in the United States one of the hottest public controversies in recent years.

2. The President announced early today that Lieutenant General Matthew Ridgway, Commander of United Nations Ground Forces, would succeed General MacArthur, effective immediately. Lieutenant General James Van Fleet is leaving tonight to take over General Ridgway's ground force command in Korea. The President said his decision to remove General MacArthur was made with deep regret. But, he said, he had concluded that General MacArthur did not wholeheartedly support United States and United Nations policies.

3. (Optional) General MacArthur has publicly advocated use of Chinese Nationalist troops against the Communists on the Chinese mainland. And he has also advocated United Nations bombing of Chinese Communist bases in Manchuria.

4. These statements of policy were made in violation of several orders, released today by the White House. (End optional)

Republican leaders in Congress immediately launched a bitter attack on President Truman and his administration, charging that the removal of General MacArthur would constitute appeasement of the Communists in the Far East. Resolutions were introduced in both houses of Congress to invite General MacArthur to appear before a joint session to express his views. Republican foreign policy leaders demanded an investigation of "the whole question of the conduct of foreign and military policy."

TEXT OF CONTROVERSIAL FORMOSA DIRECTIVE [1]

DEPARTMENT OF STATE—PUBLIC AFFAIRS AREA
POLICY ADVISORY STAFF

POLICY INFORMATION PAPER—FORMOSA

I. Problem. To formulate information policy which will minimize damage to United States prestige and others' morale by the possible fall of Formosa to the Chinese Communist forces.

II. Background. Comment on Formosa is on the increase as the Communist advances on the Chinese mainland leave the island as the last substantial part of China under Nationalist control. Attention is focused by three principal elements:

1. Communists, worldwide, who charge the United States with conspiring to build the island into a fortress to be taken over by the United States (if it does not already control it), thereby trying to brand the United States with the mark of aggressive imperialism, and also hoping to get us involved in a risky and unpromising venture;

2. Pro-Nationalists (principally in the United States) who consider Formosa a redoubt in which the government could survive, and who tend to create an impression the United States is delinquent if it fails to "save Formosa";

3. Groups in the United States who are inclined to be critical of the United States for failure to act to prevent loss of the island to the Communists, largely because of mistaken popular conception of its strategic importance to United States defense in the Pacific.

Loss of the island is widely anticipated, and the manner in which civil and military conditions there have deteriorated under the Nationalists adds weight to the expectation. Its fall would threaten:

1. Loss of United States prestige at home and abroad to the extent we have become committed in the public mind to hold it;

2. Damage to the morale of other nations, particularly in the Far East, which are disturbed by the Communist gains and fear its possible further advances.

Formosa, politically, geographically, and strategically, is part of China in no way especially distinguished or important. Although ruled by the Japanese (as "Taiwan") for fifty years, historically it has been Chinese. Politically and militarily it is a strictly Chinese responsibility.

[1] From "Text of State Department's Document on Formosa," of December 23, 1949, which was published by the Senate Committee investigating General MacArthur's removal from command. New York *Times*. 100:4. June 2, 1951. Reprinted by permission.

It is true that the technical status of the island remains to be determined by the Japanese Peace Settlement. But the Cairo Agreement and Potsdam Declaration and the surrender terms of September 2, 1945, looked to its return to China and the United States facilitated its takeover by Chinese troops shortly after V-J Day.

Even the small United States military advisory group sent there at Chinese Government request was completely withdrawn a year ago. Merely a handful of military-attaché personnel with diplomatic status remains. The United States never has had military bases there, and never has sought any special concessions there.

ECA [Economic Cooperation Administration] work done on the island, particularly through the Joint Commission on Rural Reconstruction, has been of purely economic and technical nature for assistance in improvement of conditions, and no quid pro quo has been sought.

United States public opinion has concerned itself primarily with the question of the island's strategic importance; there has been insistent demand from a few sources for military action by the United States, but it has not assumed significant proportions. Rather, public opinion obviously is divided and uncertain, and there is no apparent consensus for a particular course of active intervention.

III. Treatment. If rising public interest warrants it, gradually increasing attention may be paid Formosa, to establish publicly the facts indicated below.

Overseas use should be made of unofficial materials in public analysis and comment appearing both at home and abroad, as well as official statements as they may appear. Label conflicting public statements properly as "individual expressions of opinion," as "unofficial," etc.

All material should be used best to counter the false impressions that:

1. Formosa's retention would save the Chinese Government;
2. The United States has a special interest in or "designs on" the island or any military bases on Formosa;
3. Its loss would seriously damage the interests of either the United States or of other countries opposing communism;
4. The United States is responsible for or committed in any way to act to save Formosa.

Without evidencing undue preoccupation with the subject, emphasize as appropriate any of the following main points:

1. Formosa is exclusively the responsibility of the Chinese Government;

(a) Historically and geographically a part of China;

(b) The National Government has run the island's affairs since the takeover and is responsible for present conditions there;

(c) The United States has assumed no responsibilities or obligations, actual or moral.

2. Formosa has no special military significance;

(a) It is only approximately one hundred miles off the China coast;

(b) Other potential objects of Communist aggression are closer to points on the Chinese mainland than to Formosa;

(c) China has never been a sea power and the island is of no special strategic advantage to the Chinese Communist armed forces.

3. Economic assistance in Formosa has been for economic and social purposes, has been consistent with demonstrated United States concern for the welfare of the Chinese generally, and has involved no thought of special concessions to the United States.

4. In areas of insistent demand for United States action, particularly in the United States itself, we should occasionally make clear that seeking United States bases on Formosa, sending in troops, supplying arms, dispatching naval units, or taking any similar action would

(a) Accomplish no material good for China or its Nationalist regime;

(b) Involve the United States in a long-term venture producing at best a new area of bristling stalemate, and at worst possible involvement in open warfare;

(c) Subject the United States to a violent propaganda barrage and to reaction against our "militarism, imperialism and interference" even from friendly peoples and particularly from Chinese, who would be turned against us anew;

(d) Eminently suit purposes of the USSR, which would like to see us "substantiate" its propaganda, dissipate our energies and weaken effectiveness of our policies generally by such action.

5. In reflecting United States unofficial demands for action of various kinds in Formosa, avoid giving them prominence unwarranted by their limited (usually individual) source, and make clear that the total of such demands evidences concern and frustration in some quarters but does not add up to a consensus on any particular position different from that officially taken.

Avoid:

1. Speculation which would show undue concern with whether Nationalists can hold the island or when Communists may take it;

2. References which would indicate important strategic significance, or that the island is a political entity;

3. In output to China, any emphasis on bad conditions in Formosa under the Nationalists, although to other areas reference can be made among reasons why Nationalists are vulnerable there as elsewhere;

4. Statements that Formosa's final status still is to be determined by the Japanese Peace Treaty;

5. Name "Taiwan"; use "Formosa."

ACHESON TESTIMONY ON PURPOSE OF FORMOSA DIRECTIVE[2]

CHAIRMAN: I want the letter from the State Department. Transmitting it [the document] to the Defense Department.

May 22, 1951

My Dear Secretary Marshall: . . . Attached is a copy of Special Guidance No. 28 issued on December 23, 1949, by the policy advisory staff of the office of the Assistant Secretary of State for Public Affairs, Department of State. . . .

The series of information policy papers, of which No. 28 is one item, is designed primarily for the purpose of providing the necessary background and guidance to assist United States Government information media and United States missions abroad in interpreting major developments affecting United States foreign policy.

Such guidance is necessary in order that the government's information media may contribute effectively to the achievement of United States foreign policy objectives. Making information policy guidance public would adversely affect the conduct of the foreign relations of the United States.

Revelation of the detailed methods by which the United States conducts its foreign information program would be of assistance to the Soviets not so much in advising them of what our techniques are, but more in permitting them to take an information directive and use it for extensive counterpropaganda.

By its very nature an information policy guidance paper has to include descriptions of the various attitudes on questions and instructions on emphasis and the attitude to take in answering questions. If a copy should be made public, the USSR could use it to discredit the information program of the United States by arguing that the Voice of America is not interested in portraying truth, but rather thinks up its arguments (and by implication, its facts) as they may be necessary to support a preconceived foreign policy. . . .

Sincerely yours,

(Signed) DEAN ACHESON.

SECRETARY ACHESON: Mr. Chairman, I should like to address myself to the question of this document. It deals with information to be given out over the Voice of America to minimize the damaging effects to the United States of the possible fall of Formosa. . . . The Department of the Army, which was represented on the interdepartmental group which coordinated the information policies, suggested to the Department of State . . . that it might be very important to use the

From "Transcript of Testimony in Secretary Acheson's First Day on the Stand at Senate Hearing." New York *Times*. 100:4-7. June 2, 1951. Reprinted by permission.

Voice of America and our international techniques to minimize any damage which might occur to us in event of the fall of Formosa. . . .

First of all there were two studies made, in September and October, as to the imminence and danger of this fall. Those studies unanimously reported that the fall would occur, and would occur probably in the year 1950. . . . In the light of those studies, and those conclusions of probable fact, this document which you have before you was prepared, and, as the heading indicates, the purpose of the document was to solve the problem, if possible, of formulating policy which would minimize damage to the United States prestige and others' morale by the possible fall of Formosa to the Chinese Communist forces.

Now, I should like to explain to you the document which you have heard read. The document falls into three parts, the first part being entitled "Background." That is information solely for those men who are preparing any broadcasts or public information which is to be put out through our Voice of America. All that part of the document has nothing to do with what that person has to say.

This part of the document which begins with "Background" and goes up to the subheading "Treatment," tells the officer working on this matter what is the importance of this question, and why do we want something said about it.

It also tells him what others are saying about this subject, so that he will know the information environment into which he is about to enter. That covers all that part of the document. . . .

When we come to "Treatment," the purpose of that section is to tell him the attitude that he should take and the things that he should stress.

The final section of the paper is headed "Avoid," and that tells him things that he should not say.

Now, under the heading of "Treatment," I will not bore the committee by reading that all over again. There is very little, I think that anyone would find to quarrel with in that part of the document, with one exception, and that is—in two places it says "All material should be used to counter the false impressions that"—and one of them is that "its loss would seriously damage the interests of either the United States or other countries opposing communism."

Another place in the document is headed, under "Treatment," "The attitude shall be 'Formosa has no special military significance,'" and it gives the reasons why.

Now, it may be argued—and undoubtedly will be argued—that the policy of the United States, as I have described it, is not as stated in the parts that I have referred to.

The answer to that, the reason that we adopt this attitude, is that it is the only attitude which will have the desired effect, which is to minimize the danger to the prestige of the United States and to the morale of others should Formosa fall. . . .

I don't know any other attitude which would be sounder to take if you believed, as we did believe—and rightly believed—that an event was going to happen which would be damaging to our prestige, than to say keep your chin up, it doesn't matter, this isn't important, we will go ahead and deal with it in some other way.

That is what is behind this whole document. . . . I was just ending up by saying that, therefore, this paper that you have before you is not a paper at which you can look to prove that the State Department attitude or policy was different from that of the other branches of the government; it was not. . . .

SENATOR BRIDGES: Mr. Fisher, in his testimony. . . [stated] "In other words, the purpose of this document is, to put it crudely, give the Voice of America people the line they should follow because of an anticipated development." . . .

SENATOR SALTONSTALL: I would like to ask Secretary Acheson—this is material given to the Voice of America. How often does this confidential type of material go out to the Voice of America?

SECRETARY ACHESON: It goes out quite often.

Q: How many copies of this confidential document of December 23, 1949, under discussion were promulgated by the department?

A: . . . To missions abroad there were 234. In the Department of State 150. To other agencies 72.

Q: What in general would be the nature of the other agencies? Would that include the military?

A: National defense 42; this inter-departmental committee . . . which coordinates information 8; the CIA [Central Intelligence Agency] 20; the ECA 2. . . . I think the total is 456.

SENATOR HICKENLOOPER: Now, did copies go to all of our missions abroad?

SECRETARY ACHESON: I cannot say. I have got South America 40, Europe 90, the Far East 40, Germany, 4, the Near East 60 (Near East and Africa).

Q: Mr. Secretary, isn't it reasonable to believe that with that dissemination or promulgation of that number of copies of these documents, that this document has fallen long since into the hands of the Soviet?

A: I would not know. I should hope not. . . .

Q: Have you or does the department or the Voice of America within your knowledge or that has come to your attention—has the Soviet used this document or referred to it or the article published in the newspapers in January with reference to this document, that is January '50? Have they used it as propaganda in any way . . .?

A: We can ascertain that. I don't know it.

FURTHER TESTIMONY [3]

Q: If I understand you correctly, in discussing Special Guidance Paper No. 28, dated December 23, 1949, it was to prepare world opinion that the loss of Formosa was not really a serious blow. . . .

Mr. Secretary, how do the people out in the field, these 456 who received this so-called public relations memo know when the State Department is giving them policy or propaganda? In short, if this paper is for propaganda purposes only, where are the policy papers which back up the statement that they were fully acquainted with the fact that you considered even on December 23, 149, that Formosa was strategically important to this country?

A: . . . The people in the field are told by the heading here that this is what is known as a contingency guidance paper. That is, it is to deal with a contingency. It is quite clear to them that the contingency is not one desired, but a contingency that may occur, and where you may have to deal with it.

You asked me where the papers are which indicated the attitude of the State Department. Those are not sent out to these people in the field. Those are papers in the department itself.

PROGRAM BREAKDOWN OF VOA [4]

More than 80 separate programs, ranging from 15 minutes to one hour and amounting to approximately [41:10] program hours and about 225,000 words, are broadcast daily in 33 languages, including English, and are beamed to the *following areas*:

EUROPE

	Hrs:Mins		Hrs:Mins
German to Austria	:45	Polish	1:15
Bulgarian	:45	Rumanian	1:00
Czech and Slovak	1:15	Russian	2:00
English	6:00	Serbo-Croat	1:15
French	1:00	Slovene	:15
Finnish	:15	Spanish to Spain	:45
German to Germany	1:30	Ukrainian	:30
Hungarian	1:15	Lithuanian	:15
Italian	:15	Portuguese	:15
			[20:30]

[3] From "Transcript of Testimony at Afternoon Session of Acheson's Second Day Before Inquiry." New York *Times*. 100:8-9. June 4, 1951. Reprinted by permission.

[4] From *Fact Sheet on International Broadcasting Division*, a 4-page processed release of the Department of State, Office of International Information, February 1, 1951.

LATIN AMERICA	Hrs:Mins
English	2:15
Portuguese	:45
Spanish to Latin America	2:25
	[5:25]

NEAR EAST	
Arabic	1:00
Greek	:30
Persian	1:15
Turkish	:45
Hebrew	:30
	4:00

FAR EAST	Hrs:Mins
Amoy	:30
Cantonese	1:30
English	3:00
Indonesian	:30
Korean	1:15
Mandarin	3:00
Russian	:30
Swatow	:30
Vietnamese	:30
	11:15

TOTAL TO ALL AREAS: [41:10]

At the present time, three hours of programming to the Soviet Union (Russian and Ukrainian) is aired from the U.S.A. To counter the Soviet jamming of these programs, they are recorded at overseas relay bases and aired on a continuous basis; in effect, 24-hour service to Russia. Various other programs are rebroadcast by transcription from overseas relay bases amounting to an overall repeat total of about 47 program hours daily.

[NOTE:—The above has been corrected through April 15, 1951, but does not include the Hindi and Urdu broadcasts which were initiated May 15, 1951, or any subsequent additions or changes.—Ed.]

MAIL RESPONSE TO THE VOICE[5]

From July, 1949, to March 31, 1950, the Audience Mail Section received letters from 95,146 listeners requesting that their names be added to the permanent list to receive VOA program schedules as they are published. . . .

[111,098] letters were received from Voice of America listeners from July 1, 1949 to March 31, 1950, in the following languages:

English	21,758
French	6,915
German	44,479
German (Austria)	4,682
Italian	12,809
Spanish (L.A.)	5,010
Spanish (Spain)	8,255
Portuguese	1,850
Chinese	219
Greek	410
Others*	4,711
TOTAL	[111,098]

*Chiefly Turkish and Indonesian (2028 Turkish, 1253 Indonesian)

[5] From *The World Audience for the Voice of America,* Office of International Information and Educational Exchange, Department of State, May 1, 1950. p7-8.

BIBLIOGRAPHY

An asterisk (*) preceding a reference indicates that the article or a part of it has been reprinted in this book.

Books, Pamphlets, and Documents

Almond, G. L. American people and foreign policy. 269p. Harcourt, Brace & Co. New York. '50.

Benton, William. How we can win the peace by improving the Voice of America. 15p. Supt. of Docs. Washington, D.C.
Reprint of speech before United States Senate, February 19, 1951.

Carroll, Wallace. Persuade or perish. 392p. Houghton Mifflin Co. Boston, '48.

Chester, Giraud and Garrison, G. R. Radio and television. 550p. Appleton-Century-Crofts. New York. '50.

Childs, H. L. and Whitton, J. B. eds. Propaganda by short wave. 355p. Princeton University Press. Princeton, N.J. '42.

Doob, L. W. Public opinion and propaganda. 600p. Henry Holt & Co. New York. '48.

Dryer, S. H. Radio in wartime. 384p. Greenberg, Publisher. New York '42.

Farago, Ladislas, ed. German psychological warfare. 302p. G. P. Putnam's Sons. New York. '42.

Inkeles, Alex. Public opinion in Soviet Russia. 379p. Harvard University Press. Cambridge, Mass. '50.

*Kohler, F. D. Effectiveness of the VOA. Speech before Institute for Education by Radio-TV, Columbus, Ohio, May 4, 1951.

Kris, Ernst and Speier, Hans. German radio propaganda. 529p. Cornell University Press. Ithaca, N.Y. '44.

Lerner, Daniel. Sykewar. 463p. George W. Stewart. New York. '49.

Linebarger, P. M. A. Psychological warfare. 258p. Infantry Journal. Washington, D.C. '48.

*Macmahon, A. W. Memorandum on the postwar international information program of the United States. (Department of State Publication 2438) 135p. Supt. of Docs. Washington, D.C. '45.

Markel, Lester and others. Public opinion and foreign policy. 227p. Harper & Bros. New York. '49.

*Padover, S. K. Psychological warfare. (Headline Series no86) 65p. Foreign Policy Association. Washington, D.C. Mr.-Ap. '51.

Rolo, C. J. Radio goes to war. 293p. G. P. Putnam's Sons. New York. '42.

Thomson, C. A. H. Overseas information service of the United States Government. 397p. Brookings Institution. Washington, D.C. '48.

*United States. Advisory Commission on Educational Exchange. Trading ideas with the world; report of the Commission, March 31, 1949. (Publication 3551) (International Information and Cultural series 7) 88p. Supt. of Docts. Washington, D.C. O. '49.

United States. Advisory Commission on Educational Exchange. Two way street: 1950 report of the Commission. Supt. of Docs. Washington, D.C. '50.

*United States. Advisory Commission on Information. Semiannual report to the Congress. 19p. Supt. of Docs. Washington, D.C. Ap. '51

United States. Committee on Public Information. Reports of the chairman of the Committee for individual years, 1917, 1918, 1919. 290p. Supt. of Docs. Washington, D.C. '20.

United States. Congress. H.R. 3342; an act to promote the better understanding of the United States among the peoples of the world and to strengthen cooperative international relations. 10p. (Public law 402) 80th Congress, 2d session. Supt. of Docs. Washington, D.C. '48.

*United States. Department of State. International information program of the United States Department of State: the campaign of truth. 7p. The Department. Washington, D.C. '50.

*United States. Department of State. World audience for America's story. (Publication 3485) (International Information and Cultural series 5) 127p. Supt. of Docs. Washington, D.C. Ap. '49.

*United States. Department of State. International Broadcasting Division. Program Evaluation Branch. Report on audience mail, February, 1951. 30p. mimeo. The Department. Washington, D.C. '51.

United States. Department of State. Library and Reference Services Division. Overseas information programs of the United States government (Bibliography no58) 34p. Supt. of Docs. Washington, D.C. F. 28, '51

*United States. Department of State. Office of International Information. Fact sheet on International Broadcasting Division. 4p. The Department. Washington, D.C. F. 1, '51.

*United States. Department of State. Office of International Information. World audience for the Voice of America. 16p. The Department. Washington, D.C. My. 1, '50.

United States. Department of State. Office of Public Affairs. Foreign affairs background summary: international broadcasting. 42p. Supt. of Docs. Washington, D.C. F. '47.

United States. House of Representatives. Appropriations Committee. Department of State appropriations for fiscal year 1948; hearings before a subcommittee. 80th Congress, 1st session. Supt. of Docs. Washington, D.C. '47

United States. House of Representatives. Committee on Foreign Affairs. Survey of activities. 140p. 81st Congress, 2d session. Supt. of Docs. Washington, D.C. '50.

United States. House of Representatives. Committee on Foreign Affairs. United States information and educational act of 1947; hearings before a special subcommittee on H.R. 3342. 80th Congress, 1st session. Supt. of Docs. Washington, D.C. '47

United States. Institute of Inter-American Affairs. History of the Office of the Coordinator of Inter-American Affairs; historical reports on war administration. 347p. Supt. of Docs. Washington, D.C. '47.

United States. Office of War Information. OWI in the ETO; report on the activities of the Office of War Information in the European Theater of Operations, January 1944-January 1945. London. '45.

United States. Senate. Voice of America; joint report of a subcommittee of the Committee on Foreign Relations and the investigations subcommittee of the Committee on Expenditures in the Executive Departments. (S. Report no2) 10p. 81st Congress, 1st session. Washington, D.C. '49.

United States. Senate. Appropriations Committee. Department of State, Justice and Commerce appropriations for fiscal year 1948; hearings. 80th Congress, 1st session. Supt. of Docs. Washington, D.C. '47.

United States. Senate. Committee on Foreign Relations. Expanded international information and educational program; hearings, July 5, 6, 7, 1950, on S. Res. 343. 165p. 81st Congress, 2d session. Supt. of Docs. Washington, D.C. '50.

United States. Senate. Committee on Foreign Relations. Promoting the better understanding of the United States among the peoples of the world and to strengthen cooperative international relations; report to accompany H.R. 3342. 14p. (S. Report no811) 80th Congress, 2d session. Supt. of Docs. Washington, D.C. '48.

United States. Senate. Committee on Foreign Relations. United States information and educational exchange act of 1947; hearings on H.R. 3342 before a subcommittee. 123p. 80th Congress, 1st session. Supt. of Docs. Washington, D.C. '47.

United States. Senate. Committee on Foreign Relations. United States information service in Europe. 260p. (S. Report no855) 80th Congress, 2d session. Supt. of Docs. Washington, D.C. '48.

Warburg, J. P. Unwritten treaty. 186p. Harcourt, Brace & Co. New York. '46.

Zacharias, E. M. and Farago, Ladislas. Behind closed doors: the secret history of the cold war. 367p. G. P. Putnam's Sons. New York. '50.

PERIODICALS

*Academy of Political Science. Proceedings. 24:92-9. Ja. '51. Voice of America. F. D. Kohler

Academy of Political Science. Proceedings. 24:214-26. Ja. '51. Strategy of Soviet propaganda. H. D. Lasswell.

Academy of Political Science. Proceedings. 24:227-38. Ja. '51. Positive approach to a democratic ideology. H. J. Morgenthau.

American Foreign Service Journal. 26:11-14. N. '49. Voice of America. F. D. Kohler.

American Mercury. 71:410-18. O. '50. General Sarnoff meets the press.

*American Scholar. 20, no2:151-61. [Ap.] '51. Psychological warfare and foreign policy. S. K. Padover.

American Sociological Review. 14:221-35. Ap. '49. Nature and consequences of black propaganda. H. P. Becker.

*Baltimore Sun. p 1 F. 16, '51. Voice now stresses widening defections of Reds in Europe. R. W. Ruth.

*Billboard. 63:3. Mr. 3, '51. Washington, Paris agree: propaganda lays an egg. Ben Atlas; Art Rosett.

*Billboard. 63:1. My. 5, '51. Senators Ferguson and Green ask "Voice" reorientation. Ben Atlas

*Billboard. 63:8. My. 12, '51. Good will builder: AFRS tops "Voice's" public relations job.

*Billboard. 63:10. My. 26, '51. Ceylon transmitter.

*Changing Times. 5:24-8. My. '51. One Voice Stalin hates.

Christian Century. 66:1379. N. 23, '49. Propaganda lessons from the Russians.

Christian Science Monitor. 43:4. Je. 8, '51. Growth of Voice of America seen too fast for own good.

Christian Science Monitor Magazine Section. p5. My. 17, '47. Russia listens, to what? D. H. John.

Columbus Citizen. 53:9A. Je. 3, '51. Guided missiles may take propaganda to Red troops. D. W. Dittmer.

Commonweal. 53:53. O. 27, '50. Words for the Voice.

*Congressional Digest. 27:43-4. F. '48. Brief story of modern propaganda.

*Congressional Record. 96:3821-6. Mr. 22, '50. Struggle for the minds and loyalties of mankind—proposing a Marshall Plan of ideas. William Benton

*Congressional Record. 96:8130-1. Je. 5, '50. Vision of America. K. E. Mundt.

*Congressional Record. 96:A5552. Jl. 20, '50. Field reports of the USIE film program.

*Congressional Record. 96:13086. Ag. 21, '50. Remarks on floor of Senate. William Benton.

*Congressional Record. 96:13726-7. Ag. 26, '50. Remarks on floor of House of Representatives [criticism of news handling by the Voice of America]. John Taber.

*Congressional Record. 96:13731-2. Ag. 26, '50. Report on broadcasts concerning the Korean incident. J. J. Rooney.

*Congressional Record. 97:A1763-5. Mr. 30, '51. Reporters' roundup: how good is the Voice of America? K. E. Mundt.

Congressional Record. 97:3460-3. Ap. 5, '51. Speech before Economic Club of Detroit, February 5, 1951. Homer Ferguson.

Coronet. 29:24-9. N. '50. How to make the Russians revolt. B. F. Fellers.

Department of State Bulletin. See United States Department of State Bulletin.

Economist (London). 159:18. Jl. 1, '50. America's Voice.

Editorial Research Reports. 1:257-73. Ap. 17, '46. International information. B. W. Patch.

*Editorial Research Reports. 1:259-67. Ap. 12, '51. Non-military weapons in cold-war offensive. B. W. Patch.

*Educational Screen. 23:203-4. My. '49. Films in the U.S. information program. H. T. Edwards

*Foreign Policy Bulletin. 29:3-4. Mr. 31, '50. What should U.S. information policy try to do? V. M. Dean.

Fortune. 42:67-8. O. '50. Next Russian revolution.

*Fortune. 43:117-20. F. '51. Have we any friends?

*Harper's Magazine. 202:23-7. Ja. '51. Mumble in the Voice of America. W. H. Wells.

Infantry Journal. 60:45-51. F. '47. Paper bullet is no spitball. L. J. Margolin.

Infantry Journal. 60:30-9, 41-6. My., Je. '47. Psychological warfare in World War II. P. M. A. Linebarger.

*Information Bulletin (Office of United States High Commissioner, Germany). p 11. O. '50. "Voice of America" programs rated good.

*Information Bulletin (Office of United States High Commissioner, Germany). p2-6. D. '50. RIAS: the truth crusader. A. S. Miles.

*Institute of International Education News Bulletin. 26:7-9. Mr. 1, '51. United States information centers overseas. L. S. Morris.

Institute of World Affairs. Proceedings. 23:100-9. '46. Overseas information and cultural relations program of the Department of State. E. C. Bellquist.

Institute of World Affairs. Proceedings. 25:48-57. '48. America's answer to Communist propaganda abroad. D. H. Schneider.
International Journal. 5:31-7. Winter '49-'50. Place of broadcasting in international relations. Ian Jacob.
Journal of Social Psychology. 23:217-24. My. '46. Broadcasting to an enemy country: what appeals are effective and why. F. H. Allport and M. M. Simpson.
Journalism Quarterly. 19:349-55. D. '44. How the OWI operates its overseas propaganda machine. C. M. Hulten.
Look. 13:39. Ag. 2, '49. How to get the world on our side. J. L. Morse.
Nation. 172:51. Ja. 20, '51. Chief ingredients of cold war.
National Municipal Review. 40:12. Ja. '51. One way we are losing: winning converts to our way of thinking, regardless of cost, held more vital to safety than victory in combat. G. H. Gallup.
Nation's Business. 35:37-8. Mr. '47. What Russia is saying about us. J. B. Wood.
Nation's Business. 38:29-30. D. '50. How big is Russia's bluff? F. L. Howley.
*Nation's Business. 39:29-31. Ap. '51. Hotfoot for Stalin. P. M. A. Linebarger.
New Republic. 122:864-7. Je. 25, '47. Voice of America. Christopher Lewis.
New Statesman and Nation. 37:316. Ap. 2, '49. Peace and propaganda.
*New York Herald Tribune. 111:8. F. 17, '51. Winning the war of ideas. E. L. Bernays.
*New York Herald Tribune. 111:14. Je. 22, '51. Fighting Russian radio propaganda. Gene Gleason.
New York Times. 99:1. My. 14, '50. 100 voices beamed at Soviet planned by U.S. and Britain. James Reston.
New York Times. 99:5. Je. 11, '50. Red Radio "Voice" mapped for China. Walter Sullivan.
New York Times. 99:9. Jl. 9, '50. Radio Free Europe. Jack Gould.
New York Times. 99:7L. Jl. 25, '50. Koreans still get "Voice" broadcasts. Kenneth Campbell.
New York Times. 99:3E. Ag. 6, '50. How to win friends problem for U.S. "Voice." Arthur Krock.
*New York Times. 99:5E. Ag. 20, '50. Battle of propaganda. Robert Trumbull.
New York Times. 99:14L. S. 5, '50. Text of Eisenhower call for crusade.
*New York Times. 99:53. S. 24, '50. Mother Goose joins "cold war" on Soviet.
New York Times. 99:3. O. 9, '50. Soviet satellites set up radio bars. John MacCormac.

New York Times. 99:5. D. 26, '50. U. S. State Dept. charges U.S.S.R. propaganda verges on open psychological war.

*New York Times. 100:3. F .16, '51. More Voice news reaching Russians. Harry Schwartz.

New York Times. 100:8E. F. 18, '51. The present danger; letter to editor. R. B. Perry.

New York Times. 100:1. Ap. 6, '51. Ocean-going radio stations to waft "Voice" to the Reds. James Reston.

*New York Times. 100:4-7. Je. 2, '51. Text of State Department's document on Formosa and transcript of testimony in Secretary Acheson's first day on the stand at Senate hearing.

*New York Times. 100:8-9. Je. 4, '51. Transcript of testimony at afternoon session of Acheson's second day before inquiry.

*New York Times Magazine. p9+. Mr. 11, '51. To counter the big lie; a basic strategy. Sidney Hook.

*New York Times Magazine. p7+. Je. 24, '51. We can pierce the iron curtain. Brien McMahon.

Newsweek. 31:34. My. 22, '48. Voice of Moscow. J. B. Phillips.

Newsweek. 32:28. S. 6, '48. Building a barricade of sneers.

Newsweek. 36:48. Jl. 17, '50. Added voice: Radio Free Europe.

*Presbyterian Life. 4:8-10. Ap. 14, '51. Iron curtain is not soundproof. Harriet Rasooli-Sa'eed.

*Public Opinion Quarterly. 7:34-45. Spring '43. Fighting with information. Joseph Barnes.

*Public Opinion Quarterly. 10:582-92. Winter '46-'47. Telling the world about America. Dick Fitzpatrick.

Public Opinion Quarterly. 11:58-82. Spring '47. Hungary—proving ground for Soviet-American relations. O. W. Riegel.

Public Opinion Quarterly. 11:213-21. Summer '47. Presenting America in American propaganda. H. M. Spitzer.

Public Opinion Quarterly. 11:412-23. Fall '47. Some reasons why information campaigns fail. H. H. Hyman and P. B. Sheatsley.

Public Opinion Quarterly. 12:5-18. Spring '48. Future of psychological warfare. Hans Speier.

*Public Opinion Quarterly. 12:676-86. Winter '48-'49. Propaganda and the free society. Ralph Block.

*Public Opinion Quarterly. 14:629-66. Winter '50-'51. Propaganda to Eastern Europe. Brutus Coste.

Public Relations Journal. p33-4. D. 20, '50. America speaking. E. W. Barrett.

Same. United States Department of State Bulletin. 23:968-70 D. 18, '50

Public Relations Journal. p9-10. Ja. '51. Devices of propaganda. E. S. Bogardus.

*Public Relations News. no325. O. 2, '50.

Reporter (Fortnightly). p9-11. N. 8, '49. New key for the Voice: our propaganda could hit Russia where it hurts. Ladislas Farago.

Saturday Evening Post. 222:26-7. D. 3, '49. Falsehood: Russia's sharpest weapon. W. B. Smith.
Saturday Evening Post. 222:10. Mr. 4, '50. Must propaganda be the monopoly of the leftists?
Saturday Evening Post. 223:10. Mr. 17, '51. We must tell the Russians how they've been had.
Saturday Review of Literature. 34:7-8. F. 3, '51. Europe and the Voice of America. R. L. Shayon.
Time. 56:68. Jl. 17, '50. Urgent whisper: Radio Free Europe.
Time. 56:32. Ag. 21, '50. As they see us.
Town Meeting (Bulletin of America's Town Meeting of the Air). 15:3-15. Ap. 11, '50. Do we have an alternative to the cold war? R. E. Flanders and others.
Town Meeting (Bulletin of America's Town Meeting of the Air). 16:1-16. O. 17, '50. How should we combat Russian propaganda and distortion abroad? Owen Brewster and W. E. Givens.
United Nations World. 4:20-2. O. '50. Europe does a double-take on the United States. Louis Dolivet.
United Nations World. 5:4. F. '51. Armies, arsenals and psychological war.
United States Department of State Bulletin. 21:941-3. D. 19, '49. Propaganda: a conscious weapon of diplomacy. G. V. Allen.
United States Department of State Bulletin. 23:896-8. D. 4, '50. What the VOA does. F. D. Kohler.
United States Department of State Bulletin. 23:928. D. 11, '50. Leaflets warn Korean refugees of destruction of native towns.
*United States Department of State Bulletin. 23:945-8. D. 11, '50. Expanding techniques for a truth strategy. E. W. Barrett.
*United States Department of State Bulletin. 24:13-15. Ja. 1, '51. Stressing information themes to meet changing world conditions. E. W. Barrett.
United States Department of State Bulletin. 24:20. Ja. 1, '51. The educational exchange program—an integral part of the campaign of truth. W. C. Johnstone, Jr.
United States Department of State Bulletin. 24:55. Ja. 8, '51. Tenth Report: U.N. Command operations in Korea.
*United States Department of State Bulletin. 24:352-4. F. 26, '51. The turn of the tide. E. W. Barrett.
*United States Department of State Bulletin. 24:370-4. Mr. 5, '51. Our answer to the big lie. W. C. Johnstone, Jr.
*United States Department of State Bulletin. 24:408. Mr. 12, '51. Counteract defeatism by winning the cold war. E. W. Barrett.
*United States Department of State Bulletin. 24:409-12. Mr. 12, '51. American idea: package it for export. J. M. Begg.
*United States Department of State Bulletin. 24:639. Ap. 16, '51. Soviet big lie vs. the campaign of truth.

*United States Department of State Bulletin. 24:700. Ap. 30, '51. American national ballet theatre to tour South America.

*United States Department of State Bulletin. 24:700. Ap. 30, '51. Mass transmission of drama "Darkness at Noon" over VOA.

United States Department of State Bulletin. 24:710-11. Ap. 30, '51. Seventeenth report of U.N. Command operations in Korea.

*United States Department of State Bulletin. 24:788-96. My. 14, '51. Educational exchange among free nations.

United States News & World Report. 29:20-1. S. 29, '50. U.S. looks good to world now.

University of Chicago Round Table. p 1-18. My. 28, '50. Psychological techniques for maintaining peace; radio discussion. Walter Johnson and others.

University of Chicago Round Table. p 1-34. Ag. 20, '50. Can we defeat the propaganda of international communism? radio discussion. William Benton and others.

Variety. 82:2. Mr. 21, '51. Bonn legislators seek to halt 'Voice' over German nets.

*Variety. 82:1. Ap. 11, '51. House report says "Voice" is mismanaged.

*Variety. 82:29. Ap. 11, '51. 90% slash for "Voice" budget gets House OK.

*Vital Speeches of the Day. 16:442-4. My. 1, '50. Fight false propaganda with truth. H. S. Truman.

Vital Speeches of the Day. 17:228-31. F. 1, '51. American foreign policy. H. E. Stassen.

*World Affairs. 113:38. Summer '50. That people may speak unto people. F. A Rankin.

Speech and Debating

Competitive Debate: Rules and Strategy. By G. M. Musgrave. 151p. rev. ed. 1946. $1.25.

Discussion Methods: Explained and Illustrated. By J. V. Garland. 376p. 3d ed. rev. 1951. $3.

Extempore Speaking: A Handbook for the Student, the Coach, and the Judge. By D. L. Holley. 115p. 1947. $1.50.

High School Forensics: An Integrated Program. By A. E. Melzer. 153p. 1940. 90c.

How to Debate. By H. B. Summers, F. L. Whan, and T. A. Rousse. rev. ed. 349p. 1950. $2.75.

Representative American Speeches. By A. C. Baird, comp. Published annually in The Reference Shelf. Prices vary.

Each volume contains representative speeches by eminent men and women on public occasions during the year. Each speech is prefaced by a short sketch of the speaker and the occasion.

Selected Readings in Rhetoric and Public Speaking. By Lester Thonssen, comp. 324p. 1942. $3.